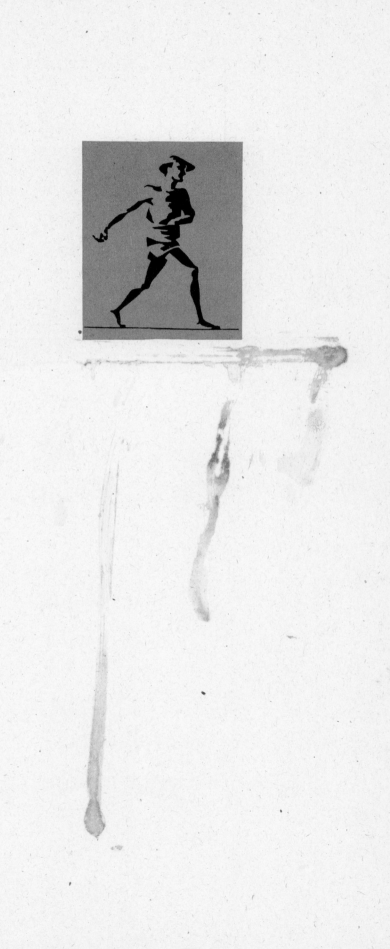

A book of practical homes for all parts of the country,

by 49 of America's Leading Architects,

containing 49 sets of plans and drawings,

together with many suggestions

for the Home Builder.

Compiled under the editorial supervision of

MARON J. SIMON

Architectural Consultant:

TALBOT HAMLIN

Professor, School of Architecture, Columbia University

Prepared with the technical assistance
and cooperation of

LIBBEY-OWENS-FORD GLASS COMPANY

YOUR

SOLAR

HOUSE

SIMON AND SCHUSTER

New York

DESIGNED BY GOBIN STAIR
SET IN CALEDONIA
THE HEADINGS ARE IMMERMAN ROMAN DESIGNED
ESPECIALLY FOR THIS BOOK
PAPER—OXFORD OFFSET FROM THE WHITAKER PAPER COMPANY
PRINTED IN THE UNITED STATES OF AMERICA BY REEHL LITHO CO., INC.
BOUND BY TRADE BINDERY

CONTENTS

CHAPTER ONE

IN THIS BOOK forty-nine of the leading architects of America present a new approach to living, a concept of a home not merely as a shelter but as an opportunity for you to expand your shelter, within the boundaries of a normal-sized building lot, until its ceiling is the sky and its front wall the far-off horizon.

These architects represent the forty-eight states and the District of Columbia. They were invited to contribute to this book as a result of their selection by a jury of men and women eminent in the field of fine arts, leaders in architecture and its related enterprises. The jurors were chosen because they are qualified to know, better than any other group, the work of the entire profession of architecture, and to select the contributors impartially and expertly.

Each of the contributing architects has created expressly for this publication a plan and design for a house inspired by his own locality, the characteristics of its people, its climate, its topography.

The only limits placed on their creations were that the houses they designed should be within the medium-priced brackets, in the localities for which they were intended, and that the houses should lift their faces to the sun through extensive windows, or even walls of glass, not only to enlist solar energy as an auxiliary heating plant but chiefly to unite interiors with the out-of-doors in a spacious, cheer-filled atmosphere.

This book presents a tremendous variety of houses and ideas for houses—houses for big lots and small lots, houses spread out or standing high, houses of new or more conventional concept. If they have any one aspect in common it is the quality which makes them "solar" houses—an open invitation to sun and sky and the spaciousness of out-of-doors to grace the days of their occupants and give them a lift in living. They enable you to take advantage of the gifts of nature which lie forever within such easy reach.

The style of building here expressed is no mere fad. It is a way of living tested for years by real American families dwelling in solar houses up and down the land. The thing that is new about this book is the unanimity with which so eminent a representation of the architectural profession has striven to put your year-round living in the sun.

How You Can Use the Book

This is a book of ideas, of suggested qualities in various types of houses. It is a book of inspirations rather than of specific patterns. It is not a house-plan book, full of pre-digested designs. It does not contain working drawings; rather its contents are detailed architectural schemes to show the relationship of room to room, room to view, to lot, to sun, to the habits of its occupants. It is unlikely that a contractor could take any set of these plans and build your house from it. But any of the ideas in this book can be adapted to your own requirements.

Some of these houses are for countryside, some for the suburbs, some for the city, some for warm climates, some for cold. Study all of them, not just the one designed for the state you live in. See what there is about each of them that you like. Your own new house can probably make use of any idea which does not go against the basic conditions under which you live.

Your home may be in Georgia, but you may take a tip from the Florida house, with its coils under glass on the roof to collect the sun's rays for heating your water supply. You may live in Nebraska, but you may want to borrow from Colorado the room arrangement that achieves what our neighbors in Mexico call a *portal*.

North Carolina's outdoor shelter, screened and glassed in, for year-round use as a game room or as a quiet retreat, may be just what you want in Iowa.

On a tight lot in populous New York you may want to adopt Mississippi's arrangement of a driveway that cuts corners and leads directly into a "carport" built diagonally to the house.

In Maine you may find it handy to borrow from Georgia the division of lavatory facilities that enables two or three persons to use the bathroom at the same time, each with complete privacy.

In Ohio you may like California's roof windows, or in Illinois you may decide to use Arizona's wading pool and wall fountain outside the bedroom, for its effect of coolness during hot weather.

Or you may like the whole house in another state and want it for your own. Just be careful that, for instance, you don't select a house developed expressly for a cold region if you live in a place where the weather usually is hot. In other words, don't buy a ski suit for a vacation in Acapulco.

Local Conditions Influence Costs

In using this book you should keep in mind that these houses were designed for the medium-priced bracket of dwelling, but their price will be influenced by the localities in which they are built. Building costs vary tremendously in different parts of the country.

The designs presented here constitute the ideas of

many of our best architects as to what the houses of today *and* tomorrow should be, the kind of living they should provide, the advantages they should offer. When you plan a solar house, go to an architect in whom you have confidence, give him all the information you can gather about the kind of house you want, so that he will know exactly what you are seeking.

Although the arrangement you need or want may not be among any of the houses developed in this book, that does not mean that you can't have a solar house. Nor does a solar house have to be a particularly expensive one. The suggestions which these designs offer will help you to express your own desires. Then your architect will be able to create for you a solar house that is definitely yours.

CHAPTER TWO

How This Book Was Launched

THE HISTORY OF ARCHITECTURE, says Le Corbusier, the eminent French architect, is a history of the struggle for light, the struggle for the window. For more than a thousand years men have striven for windows of the greatest possible size, against the limitations of construction methods and building materials and, when these were surmounted, against reactionary design influences. Eventually the window was triumphant; it won recognition not merely as an opening in a wall but as a transparent part of the wall itself.

In the 1930's, as a consequence of this victory, houses

This view, photographed at 12 noon on December 21, in solar house observed for one year by Illinois Institute of Technology, shows how the low-hanging winter sun penetrates the room.

with virtually an entire wall of glass began to dot the land-scape, oriented to accept from nature its abundant gifts of light, the welcome warmth of the winter sun, the view, the sense of oneness with the out-of-doors.

In our crisp, compartmentalized age, prone as it is to put a tag on everything, these houses, heated by the sun's rays, were tagged "solar houses."

These houses made practical use of a simple architectural principle. The most frequently used rooms for living faced the south, and the south wall was in effect one huge window. When the winter sun was low on the southern horizon its direct rays entered freely, flooding the rooms with warmth and light. In summer, when the sun was high in the heavens, its rays were barred and the house shaded by wide eaves, called "overhangs." This orientation and sun control required, of course, scientific engineering for maximum efficiency in the specific locality of each house.

Solar houses, harnessing the sun's heat, opening cheerful vistas of the out-of-doors, dispersing the sense of confinement that more conventional windows might inspire, were in themselves their own best champion.

Whenever a homeowner made a break from convention and tradition and wholeheartedly welcomed the sun and sky into his abode, his neighbors, drawn to his dwelling by normal curiosity about anything new, speculatively eyed his expansive windows. They pondered his life within four walls, one of which was glass and opened so completely onto gracious lawn or distant horizon.

Sun Heats House on Sub-Zero Day

Suddenly, in 1943, many dwellers in solar houses were blasted temporarily from the placid privacy of their normal existence. The Illinois Institute of Technology, having completed a year's observation of a solar house in the Chicago suburb of Homewood, issued its findings. The dramatic highlight of the report was an account of what happened in the house on a January day in 1942 which Chicago still remembered with shivers and shudders. The temperature dropped to 17 below zero and never rose higher than 5 below; yet automatic controls set at 72 degrees shut off the furnace at 8:30 A.M. and did not turn it on again until 8:30 P.M.! For the major part of the day the sun, streaming in through the windows which made up virtually the entire

The same room at 12 noon on June 21. Note that the sun does not enter. However, the large windows permit more daylight to enter.

south wall, had taken over the job of heating the house.

The story made the newspapers throughout the country. Chicago's colony of solar houses began to take on the aspect of a world's fair in miniature.

Reporters and cameramen raced Sunday drivers to the sites; radio interviewers sought out solar-house "authorities" and rushed them to the nearest microphones. In an article entitled "The Proven Merit of a Solar Home," the millions who devour *The Reader's Digest* drank in distilled details of the solar house, described as "the most exciting architectural news in decades." In *Life*, in *Collier's*, in *Liberty*, in *Better Homes and Gardens*, in *The American Weekly*, in the *What Cheer Chronicle*, and in *The New York Times*, in virtually every newspaper and periodical in the land, and over the nation's air waves, the praises of the solar house were sung. Motion-picture theaters from Maine to California brought the solar house alive to tens of millions in sight and sound and color.

Prospective home builders found themselves prodded on almost every hand by this new promise of an "architectural lift in living." And a glass company found itself projected by a home-hungry public into the unsolicited role of structural adviser.

Millions Seek Information

Big windows being the dominant feature of the design, a newly developed double-pane unit with which the new solar houses were glazed was mentioned frequently by its commercial name, Thermopane. For the thousands who learned of these open-faced homes and had a million questions to ask about them, this mention of Thermopane was enough to focus attention on its producer as a likely source of information. The Libbey-Owens-Ford Glass Company, of Toledo, Ohio, was swamped with thousands of letters.

These letters proceeded from the assumption that the glass company, creator of an important item in the advance of this form of housing, was expert in *all* phases of its development; they sought answers to every variety of architectural or constructional question: What should a solar house look like? How much does it cost? What materials should be used? Should the roof be flat or pitched? On what side of the street should the house be built? Was it feasible in warm sections of the country, or in cold? Could it be of one story or of two? Should it be colonial, Georgian, Spanish? What type of lot was best suited for such a house?

On the basis of such manifest interest, it was plain that a throng of Americans were interested in solar houses and presently would start building them across the land if they received even slight encouragement from any of the sources from which they sought guidance. It was also apparent that with such a trend flourishing, the company would sell acres more of glass.

This profitable prospect, however, was not received with hosannas and wild rushes for the order blanks in the offices of Libbey-Owens-Ford. For one thing, all the company's manufacturing facilities had by this time been turned over, "for the duration," to making glass for bombers, tanks, and other instruments of war. For another, the company was realistically aware that unless this new and increased use of its product sprang from a wise, skillful and apt concept and execution, the increased business thus developed would ultimately boomerang and damage its standing irreparably.

For centuries windows had been simply of a single

Even such modern buildings as the Empire State Building, tallest man-made structure in the world, otherwise employing the latest achievements of modern industry and science, have windowpanes of the single-glazed type known for centuries.

pane's thickness. Giant buildings had arisen, equipped with the newest, most modern, most efficient of mechanical devices, but with the windows that comprised half their wall areas still single-glazed in a manner that had been old when Sir Christopher Wren reared St. Paul's in the seventeenth century.

Why You May Feel Cold

It has long been an accepted fact among builders that the largest specific heat loss in a building properly insulated in every other way is through single-glazed windows.

It is a law of physics that heat flows to cold. Anyone who has sat near such a window in a warm room on a bitter winter evening has felt the twofold effects of this phenomenon. His body is chilled as its heat radiates rapidly toward the cold windowpane. Moreover, as the warm air of the room flows toward the window and is cooled by contact with the pane, it creates a chill as it rolls down the glass. To offset both the conducted loss of heat from the room and the radiant loss of body heat from persons near glass areas, radiators usually are placed near windows.

Libbey-Owens-Ford sponsored tests by independent technicians to reduce this phenomenon to plain temperature figures. The tests showed that with the outside temperature 30 below zero, the inside surface of a windowpane an eighth of an inch thick, in a room heated to 70 degrees, was only 3 degrees, and only 7 degrees if the pane were a quarter-inch thick. Under the same conditions the room surface of a Thermopane unit consisting of two eighth-inch panes sandwiching a quarter-inch air space registered 37 degrees, and the room surface of a unit of two quarter-inch panes sandwiching a half-inch air space was 42 degrees.

The problem of increasing the warmth of that inner surface of the windowpane is age-old. The Libbey-Owens-Ford company had devoted many years and a vast financial outlay to developing the double-paned, self-contained insulating window unit called Thermopane as an advance from the ancient method of glazing with single panes.

Before the development of Thermopane, one practical approach to the problem had been found in storm sash. Hung over the window at the beginning of winter and removed only at the end of the cold season, storm sash provided effective insulation despite its propensity to cloud up from condensation, frosting, and the infiltration of dirt between the panes. But as an insulator for big windows such as those the solar house demanded, storm sash was not so practical. Built to cover an unusually large window, it would be heavy and cumbersome. Oversize units would present a storage problem. Cleaning a window equipped with storm sash would mean cleaning four surfaces of glass, not two. None of these difficulties, however, would beset a double-pane unit such as Thermopane, which is in effect a unit with a self-contained storm window.

How Insulating Windowpane Works

Libbey-Owens-Ford was by no means the first to tackle the problem of a self-insulating window. The idea had been present for years and the product sought for a dozen uses— for homes, for refrigerated display cases, for locomotive-cab windows, for greenhouses, even for motorists' goggles.

The unit would consist of two panes of glass sandwiching an insulating area of dehydrated air, the whole affair

to be sealed permanently around the edges at the factory. For some installations there might be more than two panes and more than one layer of air.

An airtight seal was essential, lest moisture creep into the air layer and obscure the view through the glass by causing condensation, frosting, and etching on the inner surfaces, or lest dirt enter and settle, forever impossible to remove from these inner faces of the panes.

Experiment after experiment floundered in the same bog of bafflement; an effective seal, permanently resistant to temperature conditions and other physical variables, eluded the searchers.

Cross-sectional view of a unit of Thermopane.

With such rigid seals as they could make, the expansion and contraction of glass under the strain of temperature changes cracked the panes or sheared them away from the seal. With flexible seals they devised, the bonds loosened and moisture and dirt crept into the air spaces.

In 1930 technicians under Dr. George B. Watkins, Libbey-Owens-Ford research director, inspired by an air-conditioning problem in one of their own plants, started a long series of attempts to design a satisfactory double-pane glass unit. In the same year, Charles Haven, a Milwaukee refrigeration engineer, started an independent quest for the same thing. As did all their predecessors, Haven and the glass-company technicians bogged down on the seal to hold the two glass panes together. Haven managed to bond celluloid strips to two glass panes and removed the moisture from the space between. He named the product Thermopane, and began manufacturing it in his basement. The bond failed in actual use, however; it was too rigid.

In 1934 the company and Haven joined forces. Libbey-Owens-Ford bought his firm and product and engaged his services. Research by the Mellon Institute in Pittsburgh, under a fellowship established by the glass company, eliminated products of the organic world as possible materials for a satisfactory bond. Haven, simultaneously, headed a drive to develop a metal seal, and ultimately succeeded. This research established that melted lead, or solder, was the proper adhesive. Then the glass company's investigators set out to find an effective metal binder.

After unsuccessful experiments with hundreds of alloys, they demonstrated in 1937 that aluminum, titanium, and copper combined to yield the long-sought bond. Ninety times a Thermopane unit sealed with this alloy was subjected to, and survived, tests it would never have to meet in actual use. These tests consisted of subjecting the unit to mechanically created weather cycles of exaggerated severity. Each cycle consisted of twenty-four hours of dry atmosphere at 150 degrees, an atmosphere of saturated steam at 145 degrees for the next twenty-four hours, then a full day at 20 below zero. Most of the other alloys withstood only eight or ten such cycles.

The successful seal had a tensile strength of 800 to 1000 pounds to the square inch. The first commercial shipment of Thermopane with a metal-to-glass bond was made in November, 1937.

Having perfected its product only after such travail, Libbey-Owens-Ford was loath to introduce it to the public through any but the most responsible usage. The long and difficult struggle for Thermopane was intended to provide a successful double-glass window unit for picture windows, for general application in all types of buildings, and for various commercial uses, such as refrigerated display cases. But its performance had been most spectacularly dramatized in the solar house. Thermopane had been identified as the windowpane for solar houses in virtually all the tremendous publicity which these houses generated. Moreover, solar housing was undeniably a vast potential market for the product.

But the solar house, with its sharp break from tradition, its rigid requirements for correct orientation, exact overhangs, and other scientific elements, was likewise a potentially dangerous market unless its whole school of design

was guided by faithful, competent preceptors who would make it a true contribution to better living.

Every solar house, the company knew, represented an individual problem in engineering and planning. For example, failure to co-ordinate the mechanical heating plant of the house with the heat of the sun could turn the house into an oven or an icebox. Or improper placement of the structure could face it to a repulsive view or strip it of privacy. Or miscalculation of overhangs might well enough bar direct solar rays in June, when the sun was at its highest point, but admit them to the house in August or September, when the sun was lower in the sky but the temperature was still so high that solar heat was as welcome as a toothache.

These errors would make the solar house a failure, bringing the owner's wrath down not alone on the design but on the very materials, item by item, of which the house was built. In such an application Thermopane, for all its proved merit, would suffer an undeserved reverse.

Recognizing that these architectural problems were primarily the logical function of the architectural profession, secondarily the responsibility of manufacturers of building products, Libbey-Owens-Ford determined to launch a program sponsoring the creation of designs for sound, acceptable solar houses which could be demonstrated to the public under a wide variety of climatic or geographical conditions.

To this end the company sought to have an architect in each state and in the District of Columbia design a solar house to fit the needs, background, and environment of his own locality.

These designs, the company hoped, would serve as a stimulus to the development of a type of contemporary architecture which would be not only functional but pleasing in character. It must be immediately acceptable to the average home builder who by instinct and tradition might be inclined to favor forms less suitable to contemporary needs. Being a realistic business enterprise, the company also hoped that this type of architecture would open up a new, well-guided and responsible market for a product which had already established its usefulness in other fields.

With the Libbey-Owens-Ford Glass Company, as with every manufacturer of quality building material, the success of *all* architects is a matter of real concern and the good will of all is an obvious asset.

Determined, for the sake of the program's effectiveness, to commission architects on the basis of their proved ability and progressive ideas, the company was equally determined, for reasons of sheer tact, to have nothing whatever to do with selecting one architect over another in any given locality. It hit upon a completely impartial plan that, in the opinion of the publishers of this book, has resulted in assembling a pre-eminent volume of architectural skill.

The glass company enlisted the leaders of the field of fine arts, men and women most familiar with the work of the architectural profession in all parts of the country, to serve as a panel which would nominate the designers of the forty-nine solar houses. The nominees, chosen without any influence by the company, would be accepted without question by Libbey-Owens-Ford and offered commissions to execute the designs.

Famous Authorities Selected Architects

For their assistance to the cause of better housing and fuller living, the services of the following men and women who served on the nominating panel are gratefully acknowledged:

Leopold Arnaud, New York, dean of the School of Architecture, Columbia University

Raymond J. Ashton, Salt Lake City, former president, American Institute of Architects

Jean Austin, New York, editor, *The American Home*

Turpin C. Bannister, Auburn, Ala., dean of School of Architecture and the Arts, Alabama Polytechnic Institute

Harold Bush-Brown, Atlanta, head of the Department of Architecture, Georgia School of Technology

Walter L. Doty, San Francisco, editor, *Sunset Magazine*

Dorothy Draper, New York, industrial designer and decorator

John Entenza, Los Angeles, editor, *Arts and Architecture*

Katherine Morrow Ford, New York, architectural editor, *House & Garden*

Edward G. Gavin, Chicago, editor of *American Builder*

Robert P. Gerholz, Flint, Mich., past president, National Association of Home Builders of the U. S.

Mary Davis Gillies, New York, interiors and architectural editor, *McCall's Magazine*

Elizabeth Gordon, New York, editor, *House Beautiful*

Arthur P. Herrman, Seattle, executive officer, School of Architecture, University of Washington

W. F. Hitchens, Pittsburgh, professor of architecture, Carnegie Institute of Technology

Caleb Hornbostel, D.P.L.G.R.A., New York, consulting architect, *Woman's Home Companion*

George Howe, Philadelphia, former deputy commissioner for design and construction, Federal Works Agency, Public Buildings Administration

Joseph Hudnut, Cambridge, Mass., dean of the Graduate School of Design, Harvard University

Dexter W. Johnson, Portland, Ore., managing editor, *Western Building*

Roy Jones, Minneapolis, professor and head of the School of Architecture, University of Minnesota

George S. Koyl, Philadelphia, professor of architecture and dean of the School of Fine Arts, University of Pennsylvania

Ernest Langford, College Station, Tex., head of the Department of Architecture, Agricultural and Mechanical College of Texas

Maxine Livingston, New York, family home editor, *Parents' Magazine*

Sherley W. Morgan, Princeton, N. J., director of the School of Architecture, Princeton University

Frederick V. Murphy, Washington, head of the Department of Architecture, Catholic University of America

Howard Myers, New York, publisher, *Architectural Forum*

John Normile, A.I.A., Des Moines, Ia., building editor, *Better Homes & Gardens*

Warren C. Perry, Berkeley, Calif., dean of the School of Architecture, University of California

Richard Pratt, New York, associate editor, *Ladies' Home Journal*

Kenneth Reid, New York, editorial adviser, *Progressive Architecture*

Walter T. Rolfe, Austin, Tex., former chairman of the Department of Architecture, and professor, University of Texas; now of Goleman & Rolfe, Houston and Beaumont, Texas

Harold H. Rosenberg, Chicago, editor-publisher of *Practical Builder*

Henry H. Saylor, Washington, editor, *Journal of the American Institute of Architects*

Francis de N. Schroeder, New York, editor, *Interiors*

Howard Leland Smith, Washington, architectural adviser, underwriting division, Federal Housing Administration

Arthur McK. Stires, Pemaquid, Me., architectural writer

Kenneth K. Stowell, New York, editor, *Architectural Record*

William W. Wurster, Cambridge, Mass., dean of the School of Architecture and Planning, Massachusetts Institute of Technology

Every member of the panel was asked to nominate at least one architect for each state. The architects were to be, in the judgment of the nominator, well qualified to interpret in terms of contemporary architecture a solar house which would be in keeping with the general environment, and the geographic and climatic conditions, of their respective states.

Cost Was Only Limitation

To each of the architects chosen in their respective states, the Libbey-Owens-Ford Glass Company offered a commission to design a solar house. A flat fee was paid to architects commissioned, simply to develop a plan and execute designs. The company did not dictate the cost of the house. The only limit placed on cost was that it should not exceed $15,000, by prewar standards, in the locality for which the house was intended.

When Libbey-Owens-Ford undertook this project its intention was primarily to make the resulting information available as an assistance to all architects, to contractors, to heating and ventilation engineers, and to all others engaged in the building industry.

As there was nothing secret about the program except the nomination of the participating architects, Simon and Schuster, among others, learned of it. As publishers they readily recognized that the material compiled in this project was valuable not only to architects, professional builders, and real-estate enterprises, but to every man and woman who wanted to build a home. Consequently this book was published for all, in the interest of good housing.

CHAPTER THREE

The Fight for Light

THE QUESTION this book poses to the prospective home-owner is not how he will choose as between "traditional" and "modern" or whether he will elect "colonial" or "Georgian" or "Tudor" or "classic-revival" or "Spanish" for his home. It is simply how he will take advantage of present-day materials and methods for home building against the background of his intellectual, emotional, and aesthetic nature, in order to make his house an enduring inspiration and satisfaction for those whom it shelters.

The history of the architecture of homes is one great chronicle of man's attempt to shelter himself from his hostile environment. When man evolved upon the earth (when, as anthropologists say, he came down from the trees), he faced a hostile world—wild beasts, numbing cold, enervating heat, drenching rains, and bitter winds. To escape them he went into a cave—dark, dirty, difficult to clean. Presently he emerged to a hut. Both cave and hut were windowless and dark. There was no material at hand to keep the weather out and let light in at the same time.

Being, however, a heliocentric, or light-loving, animal, he sought a means by which to admit light. In primitive homes he brought it in through the doorway and the smoke outlet of the roof. It was the beginning of that centuries-long struggle for light, that struggle for the window, which constitutes the history of architecture.

Wanted—Heat AND Shelter

Presently the primitive householder achieved the effect of a window in the wall; he modified his door to a hatch or half-door arrangement, by which he gained a certain amount of illumination and protection against the weather at the same time.

We may reasonably assume that these first "windows," wall or roof openings, were covered with animal skins or cloth, supplanted much later by translucent stone, such as gypsum or translucent sheets of marble, or by shells, mica, or alabaster.

Eventually, probably in the second millennium before the time of Christ, glass was discovered, its exact birth still a matter of conjecture, its history full of romance and violence. With its discovery man had an increasingly efficient means of admitting light to his home while excluding from it the hostile weather.

Probably the first people to use glass for windows were the Romans, who learned its manufacture from the Egyptians when Egypt became a province of their empire. The Romans, however, exploited glass chiefly for decorative purposes, and its development was not sufficient to displace stone, cloth, or shells entirely as a window covering.

Glassmaking Was Secret Art

The Romans did, however, civilize western Europe, and there presumably distributed the craft of glassmaking. Glass, one of the oldest known of man-made materials, was cloaked in mystery and black magic for centuries, when even murder was an instrument to protect the secret of its manufacture. Its production was carried on behind closed doors and guarded by secret guilds whose members were put to death and their families thrown into prison for any slightest disclosure of the secrets of their art.

It is a logical deduction that the use of glass for windows received great impetus from the spread of civilization to the west, where greater protection against the weather was needed; lumps and pools of glass found in the ruins of burned Roman villas in England prove its use for windows there. But glass was still a precious item that only the rich and powerful could use.

During the early Middle Ages the Church became rich. In a time of widespread ignorance and warfare, it served as the beacon of civilization. It was natural that the Church turned early to the use of glass for windows in the host of edifices it erected, and out of small pieces of colored glass held together by lead strips there developed gradually an art of great power—the art of stained glass. Thus large windows came more and more into use, and flooded the churches with colored light.

But the use of glass for homes was still economically impossible and far away. Small single panes in shutters, or tiny pieces of leaded glass, began to appear in French town houses of the late twelfth century. In England it was not until the thirteenth century that we find a record of the use of glass in houses, in commands of Henry III to install glass windows in some of his residences. Not until the latter years of the sixteenth century, however, when it ceased to be a luxury and became economically available to the well to do, was there a truly extensive use of glass for domestic windows.

Windows formed of numerous small panes became more and more frequent all over Europe, and in England especially they grew larger and larger until sometimes they formed the entire side of a room, except for the piers which supported the wall. The enormous gain in illumination thus achieved accounts for the development of decorative furniture in the seventeenth century; now that furni-

The hall windows of Ockwells Manor, Berkshire, England, an example of late
fifteenth-century architecture in England.　　　—Copyright, Country Life, London.

ture could be seen so readily it was made richer and more
luxurious.

Taxes Held Down Size of Windows

It was, however, only a temporary victory in the ancient
struggle of windows to achieve greater dimensions. Com-
promises to current fashions, limitations of structural materials, considerations of heating requirements kept them
down; the tax on windows, in force in England from 1695
until the middle of the last century, and in America in colonial times, made them a costly indulgence.

As old as the window itself is the knowledge that we
need not fight nature in the planning of our houses but can
co-operate with it and use natural ventilation and the heat
of the sun to our great profit, economically and emotion-
ally.

Vitruvius, the celebrated Roman architect and engineer,
who lived about the time of the birth of Christ, commented
on it in his *Ten Books of Architecture*, dedicated to his em-
peror, Augustus, in which he noted how "the special purposes of different rooms required different exposures suited
to convenience and to the quarters of the sky."

Three hundred years earlier, Xenophon had written:
"In houses with a south aspect, the sun's rays penetrate into
the porticoes in winter, but in summer the path of the sun
is right over our heads and above the roof, so that there is
shade. If, then, this is the best arrangement we should build
the south side loftier, to get the winter sun, and the north
side lower to keep out the cold winds."

Making Nature Work for Man

The idea of making nature work for man in housing controlled folk building in many early nations. A vivid example is the Persian *iwan*, an open porch exposed to the south
and surrounded by buildings on the other three sides. It
served as an outdoor sitting room sheltered from cold
winds and comfortable in the light and heat of the sun.

In later times, however, the ancient lesson was long

15

John Ward House, Salem, Massachusetts, after 1684.

rejected or ignored. For centuries military considerations inspired the builders of many houses—the main concern with defense rather than with livability; narrow apertures from which to hurl weapons took precedence over broad windows through which to admit light.

Thus back and forth the struggle of the window raged, winning a brief victory in Gothic, flaring up again in Renaissance, achieving scattered triumphs in the eighteenth century in houses now regarded as classic examples of fenestration.

In the latter decades of the nineteenth century big windows—"picture windows" that seemed to bring the outdoors into the house—found stanch champions in the designers of the summer houses that began to rise in America's mountain-lake and seashore resort communities.

These houses, closely integrated with their sites, flexible, daring in their use of free space, minimizing partitions between rooms, were prophetic of a trend, but one which

would be of distant flourishing. This uniquely American style died prematurely under the onslaught of twentieth-century worship of old architectural forms combining with an age in which the focus of summer holidaying swung from the country home to the country club and the automobile.

Meanwhile, however, from the 1890's, the Chicago architectural school waged an unremitting campaign for houses of clear, simple design which would wed interiors and exteriors and would no longer be mere enclosures that shut out the world. In the late 1920's their preachments began to take root.

Making Homes More Livable

The houses that stemmed from this school were modern, but not in the sense that modern is taken to mean defiance of convention and accepted tradition—not a deliberate flying in the face of tradition. Rather they were modern in the

16

sense that architecture has never been static, that throughout the long succession of the generations there have been architects who dedicated themselves to designing in new ways with the sole aim of increasing the livability of their houses and establishing for the dwellers therein more complete emotional fulfillment.

At the same time a new appreciation developed in this country for the daring new kinds of houses that the best architects in Europe were building. It was seen that these houses, called "radical" at the time, had a freedom of plan, a logic of arrangement, for better and easier housekeeping and living. In them, too, glass played an enormous part, and great undivided panes were often a marked feature in their design. The designers were attempting to develop a new kind of house based on twentieth-century living and twentieth-century building materials.

New materials, new industrial processes, open new approaches to all endeavors. The development of the steam engine, the gasoline engine, jet propulsion, set up new concepts of transportation. The development of the sulfonamides made possible new therapies against disease. The invention of wireless recast the communications system of the world.

So in architecture, it is a long-accepted truth that new materials and new building methods result in new forms of architectural beauty. And many materials may well be regarded as new if they are old materials come within the range of a larger number of pocketbooks. The production of steel, reinforced concrete, glass, brought about new styles, new methods of construction. For example, windows composed of many small panes held together by a crisscross of muntin bars were forced upon all but wealthy homeowners until comparatively recent years simply because it was not until this century that methods were devised for the production of large sheets of good-quality window glass at a price within the reach of all.

The intellectual, aesthetic, and emotional nature of the dweller within a house is as important a consideration as the

Windows can integrate the indoors and the outdoors as parts of a single experience.

practical, physical problems which the designer of the house must solve. Clearer and clearer has become the recognition of so many men's desire to have their homes combine the actuality of shelter with the feeling of outdoor nature. The severe tensions of modern life demand serenity of a house as an antidote for the pressure of factory or office.

Interest Grows in Solar Architecture

This desire for the integration of the indoors and the outdoors as parts of a single experience began to achieve gradually more extensive fulfillment in the late 1920's and the 1930's. Great emphasis began to be placed on means of eliciting nature's co-operation and using natural ventilation and solar heat to great advantage.

The market was there. The scientific means of satisfying it likewise were at hand. In this country and abroad, architects and city planners, confronted with the prospect of erecting gigantic housing developments, were making detailed, scientific studies of the sun's daily and seasonal procession across the sky, intent on learning how best to orient in order to win from the sun all possible illumination for the multitude of rooms within the walls of the massive housing projects they contemplated. It was but a short step

to extend these studies to investigate control of the sun's direct rays, long known to designers and constructors of greenhouses as the world's most vigorous source of heat for building interiors. In short, a study of solar housing arose.

A solar house, fundamentally, is a house designed to attain more efficient use of the sun for heat and natural daylight, and to achieve better vision. Through glass walls on southern exposures the radiant energy of the winter sun, as it swings low on southern horizons, is admitted to the house and warms it. In summer, when heat is a burden, overhanging roof constructions keep out the direct rays of the high-riding sun.

The three basic considerations in the design of a solar house are: orientation, use of large windows, control of the sun's rays.

Orientation, in the language of the architect, means the laying out of a plan in relation to specific elements, such as the position of the sun and the prevailing direction of the wind. In solar housing north of the equator it means facing as many rooms as possible to the south to obtain the benefits of solar radiation in winter.

Large windows are necessary to provide entry of solar radiant energy in winter months. Large windows mean

Windows permit the eye of the dweller within the house to travel to distant scenes now closely joined with the enclosure in which he lives. *Architect: James F. Eppenstein.*

wide views, so the surroundings of the house should be considered with the idea of producing the most pleasant view; in turn, existing views will affect the position of windows. Landscaping is an integral part of the solar-house plan, and should be undertaken to enhance the view, to provide screening for privacy when required, and sometimes to furnish shade in summer heat.

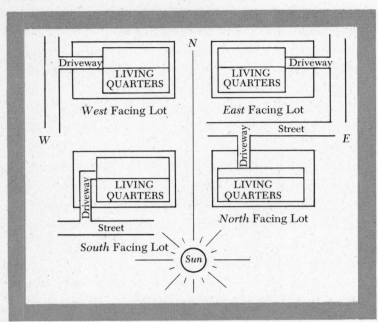

This simplified sketch shows the fundamentals of orienting or planning living areas to face the sun. Such orientation cannot be accomplished in every instance, there being literally thousands of different conditions existing because of lot sizes—front footage limitations, hilly land, etc. However, the four sketches suggest some of the possibilities of facing the main rooms—if only the living room—south regardless of which direction the lot faces. Try out this idea with your own lot in mind.

Roof Overhangs Control Sun's Rays

Sun control is achieved by the use of permanent or temporary roof overhangs, visors, and other opaque surfaces to regulate shadow areas on windows so that sunlight may enter during cold weather and be shut out during warm.

The sun, in the arc it describes each day from rising to setting, is at its highest point at noon. As the earth tilts on its axis there is a great winter-summer variation in the sun's position in relation to the southern horizon. At Chicago, for instance, the sun at noon on June 21 stands almost overhead at 71.5 degrees; at noon on December 21 it has dropped to 24.5 degrees, a variation of 47 degrees.

North of the equator the sun is in the southern sphere. A solar window faces south. Above it the roof has been extended or a visor hung, as if it were a brim on a hat. It is apparent that in a season of scorching temperatures the rays of the high summer sun are blocked by the hat brim of the house. But they pour beneath it into far reaches of the room when the sun rides 47 degrees lower in the winter sky and its warmth is a welcome friend.

Roof extensions may be a permanent, integral part of the house, or they may be movable. They may be designed to be taken down in the fall, if local conditions indicate. Overhangs may consist of slats tilted to permit the flow of air and the entry of light but to screen out the direct rays of the sun. They may be designed as trellises, with wide leaves of plants growing over them in summer as a sunshade.

Since the heat of the sun serves as an auxiliary to the mechanical heating system of the house, the solar and the mechanical heat must be co-ordinated through thermostatic controls. Size of overhangs must be calculated on the length of the hot season, the recorded positions of the sun, and the latitude in which the house is built. In the hands of capable professionals both the co-ordination of heating and the planning of overhangs are simple problems to solve. The man who builds a solar house should assign competent architects and heating engineers to solve them.

Double-Pane Window Cuts Heat Losses

Dependence on solar heat has posed a dilemma all

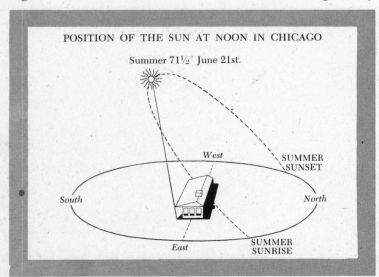

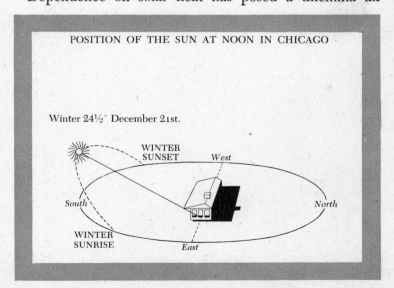

These three diagrams show how roof extensions serve to control the entry of the direct rays of the sun in a solar house in a specific location. The seasonal tilting of the earth accounts for the high and low paths of the sun in summer and winter.

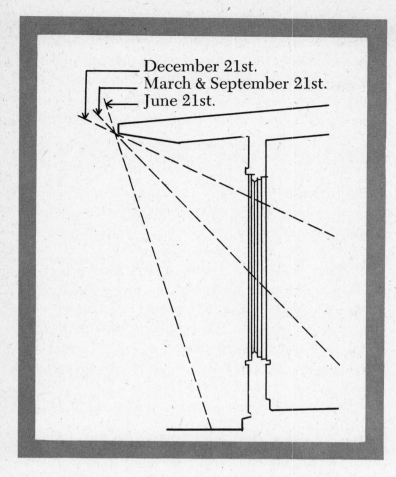

December 21st.
March & September 21st.
June 21st.

How overhanging eaves in a solar house admit or keep out the direct rays of the sun at various seasons of the year.

through the ages of single-pane windows. The heat gained from the sun may be more than offset by heat losses through the single or uninsulated panes. The double-pane window cuts down these losses while still permitting the entry of solar heat as a gain.

Even though the sun may be obscured, it is functioning as a heating auxiliary for the solar house. Its contribution is measured thus by a United States Weather Bureau investigator of solar radiation: "Assuming the heat value of a clear day to be 100 per cent, from 60 to 80 per cent as much should be received on hazy days, and from 5 to 50 per cent might be expected on dull days."

The records of the Federal meteorological service also establish that there is more sunshine in winter than most people realize as they skid in cold discomfort through snow and slush. Weather records covering more than thirty years in eleven Northern and Midwestern cities, chosen at random, show sunshine for at least half the total of possible daylight hours between September 15 and June 15.

To provide a comparison of the cost of heating solar houses and conventional dwellings Purdue University, under a grant from Libbey-Owens-Ford, built two houses on its Housing Research campus which were identical except for their respective glass areas, and conducted exhaustive tests in them.

Researchers Find Seasonal Savings

Preliminary results of these research investigations have been published in technical journals and in the transactions of engineering societies. Architects and heating engineers now employ them to help homeowners use solar windows with maximum effectiveness and to take full advantage of "the seasonal saving that in most localities accompanies the use of large glass areas in south walls."

With extensive glass exposures an integral part of solar-house design, so much concern with the sun as an auxiliary heating plant and with control of its direct rays on hot days is practical and necessary.

People who live in solar houses, however, usually chose solar design for the livability it affords. Although no normally provident person is averse to saving on his heating or illumination costs, these dwellers in the sun select their open houses, with big windows admitting the fullest quota of daylight, more from psychological than economic motives.

Only as they are measured against the history of architecture are such houses new. Actually there are scores of them throughout the country, completed and occupied for several years before the war. (Indeed, there has been little private home building since December 7, 1941.) They are found in such varying localities as Long Island and Cleveland and Chicago and southern California. Their occupants, likewise, form as varied a group.

There is, for instance, Rudolph Teichner, a mechanical engineer in charge of plant layout for the Western Electric Company, whose house in Roslyn, Long Island, built in 1941, represented the first incursion of "modern," not to say "solar," architecture into his village. He is impatient in his explanation of his choice of such a house:

"You wouldn't buy a 1912 car today if you could get a 1947 model, would you? Houses are just like cars. The new models are better—better building materials, better design ideas, better construction methods. It's just a better way to live than we knew in 1912."

He had two main objectives on plan when he built his house: "We knew we wanted the living room in back and the kitchen in front, and we wanted to face the house into the sun and open it up with big windows. We found the plot we wanted, planned the house to fit the plot, and then landscaped it to give ourselves the views and the privacy we wanted."

"It's a Grand Place to Live"

There is Lambert Ennis, professor of English at Northwestern University, who built a solar house in staid, conservative Evanston, Illinois.

"I never think of the economies of the house but I have

been struck with the thought that it's better for the morale—keeps you cheerful and in good disposition," he says. "If you say any one thing about a solar house it's the fact of its livability. It's a grand place to live."

Not far away, in Glenview, Illinois, is the solar house of

Living room of solar house of Robert Sidney Dickens in Glenview, Ill. *Architect: Arthur Purdy.*

Robert Sidney Dickens, a Chicago designer of industrial products, who thinks savings on light and fuel are the smallest advantages of such a house.

"You'll feel and appreciate this kind of house more in other ways—more important ways," he says. "When we built this house we wanted comfort most of all, and convenience. We wanted freedom of space and vision, spacious and sunny rooms, the sweep of the outdoors."

The occupants of solar houses have learned another and tangible advantage. Indoors they can grow plants luxuriantly and hardily, and plants are an integral part of design in modern architecture; they are living adornments, giving vitality, variety, and continual change to interiors, supplanting and surpassing the ornamentation of heavier décor.

Styles in Housing for America

No better testimonial to an architectural style may be found than in the degree to which that style anticipates or satisfies the demands of the families whose houses it will govern.

In April, 1945, the magazine *Architectural Forum,* an eminent and expert publication in the building field, devoted its issue to a "House Omnibus" to determine what those demands might be. The omnibus consisted of a digest of the architectural presentations of seven magazines, *Better Homes and Gardens, Country Gentleman, House Beautiful, Ladies' Home Journal, McCall's, Parents' Magazine,* and *Woman's Home Companion,* having a combined circulation of more than 17,000,000.

More than two thirds of the presentations dealt with the style of architecture which merges out-of-doors with interiors, opens walls through wide glass expanses, and permits the eye of the dweller within the house to travel to distant scenes now closely joined with the enclosure in which he lives.

The periodicals which originally carried those presentations are consumer magazines. They are magazines for and of the families of Messrs. Teichner and Dickens and Ennis and millions of other Americans who share their pride of home and their desire for a pleasant place to live. They follow, or anticipate, or influence the tastes of their readers. While even their editors would scarcely claim infallibility as polls of public opinion as to architectural style, their weight of evidence plainly indicates that modern architecture certainly is on the march, that houses such as the following forty-nine will rise across the land in growing numbers.

ANSWERS TO QUESTIONS MOST OFTEN ASKED ABOUT SOLAR HOUSES

Q: What does a solar house cost?
A: No more than any other well-constructed house of comparable size. The cost of a solar house, just as that of any other, is determined by such conditions as its size, the kind of building materials and the construction methods used, local labor costs, and other factors, such as equipment and fixtures, depending on the tastes and desires of the individual owner.

Q: Can I get a bank loan on a solar house?
A: As collateral for a loan a solar house is generally regarded in the same category as any other type of home, and receives from banks the same consideration as a more conventional style of house in equal location and of equal quality. A number of banking publications have featured articles about the solar house, and a great many banks and loan associations have actually displayed scale-model solar houses in their lobbies.

Q: Are light bills high or low in a solar house?
A: In a solar house whose occupants take advantage of the greater amount and longer hours of natural daylight brought in by the large windows, light bills are obviously lower than in a house with fewer and smaller windows. If the natural daylight is duplicated by profligate use of artificial illumination, the opportunity for saving on the light bill will be lost. But solar-house dwellers usually turn on their artificial lights far later than their neighbors do, and use them far less in the early morning.

Q: How do I start planning a solar house?
A: Start with this book. Study all the ideas which it presents. Decide which ones you like. Watch the architectural and home-planning magazines and books on contemporary architecture for further ideas. Then retain an architect in whom you have confidence, tell him everything you can about the kind of house you want, let him know exactly what you are seeking, so that he can adapt your ideas and desires when he drafts the working plans from which your house will be built.

Q: Can any builder erect a solar house?
A: Any competent builder can erect a solar house. He does not have to plan it. He simply has to follow your architect's blueprints.

Q: What type of lot must be used for a solar house?
A: Many types of lots may be used for solar houses. This book lists houses planned for corner lots, for inside lots, for flat or hilly terrain, for city, suburb, or country. The number of rooms which may be exposed to the sun varies, of course, in relation to the available footage facing south. For example, a lot extending 100 feet from east to west permits a southern exposure, on each floor, of more rooms than a lot half that wide would allow. A two-story house on a narrow lot naturally permits orientation of more space to the south.

Q: What materials must I use for my solar house?
A: Your choice is governed only by what you want and can afford, in keeping with the style of house which you select. Give careful consideration to your architect's opinion.

Q: Can I have a solar house in the latitude in which I live?
A: Yes. Carefully planned overhangs, sensible ventilation, and a mechanical heating system devised to function in co-ordination with the heat of the sun make the solar house as widely practical as any other type of house. In climates so warm no mechanical heating system is necessary, the solar house is attractive for its charming views of the out-of-doors and its general invitation to more cheerful living.

Q: Does it matter which way my lot faces?
A: No. The property need not face the south to achieve southern exposure of the main rooms for living. Although houses customarily have been faced to the street, it has become a widely accepted fact that this is by no means necessary or even "best." Frequently there are many advantages in turning a house away from the street. Lot sizes, front footage, hilly land, and many other conditions will govern the number of rooms which may be faced to the south on any lot, but on almost every piece of property the living room, at least, can achieve southern exposure.

Q: Is diversity of style possible in solar houses?
A: It certainly is. Just review the house designs published in this book. A solar house is not a "modernistic" house. It is a modern house, taking advantage of modern materials and building methods and the benefits they afford. Its exterior appearance may be only little different from more traditional houses, or it may assume a newer architectural form.

Q: If I build a solar house, how can I be sure that the overhangs and orientation are correct?
A: Choose a competent architect and leave it up to him. Calculation of overhangs, determination of orientation, are scientific, engineering problems individual to each house. In the hands of capable professionals they can be accurately resolved.

Q: Must a solar house be a one-story house?
A: No. Whether your solar house is of one story or two stories will be determined by your personal desires and needs and the conditions of the property on which you are going to build.

Q: Can a solar house have a basement?
A: Yes. Whether it has a basement or not depends on the owner's wishes. Some find it uneconomical to excavate for a basement, others want the facilities it may house placed below the first floor.

Q: Do I plan the landscaping when I plan the house?
A: Planting provides shade and view for the occupants of a solar house, sometimes is used to create a screen for privacy; it should be specified in detail as an integral part of the house plan. Solar housing enables you to make use of your entire lot as a place for living; the house itself is merely an enclosure which provides shelter.

Q: What type of heating should I have in my solar house?
A: This is a matter to be worked out with your architect. Just be sure that it is installed in consultation with a competent heating engineer to co-ordinate your mechanical heating plant and the heat of the sun through thermostatic controls.

Q: Is it expensive to heat a solar house?
A: A comparsion of the costs of heating solar houses and houses of conventional design was investigated by Purdue University under actual conditions. Results of the study, according to an announcement of the investigators, show "seasonal saving that in most localities accompanies the use of large glass areas in south walls." After a year's test of a solar residence in suburban Chicago, the Illinois Institute of Technology reported: ". . . The

preponderance of evidence indicates that the solar-heat input in the house tested offset most, and probably all, of the heat losses through the extra window areas."

Q: *Isn't a solar house cold on a cloudy winter day?*

A: No. Not only do you have your mechanical heating plant, but even though the sun is obscured it still functions as a heating auxiliary for the solar house. A United States Weather Bureau investigator of solar radiation says: "Assuming the heat value of a clear day to be 100 per cent, from 60 to 80 per cent as much should be received on hazy days, and from 5 to 50 per cent might be expected on dull days."

Q: *Can I heat my solar house entirely by the sun?*

A: Only if your house is in a sufficiently warm climate. A properly constructed and ventilated house is not a heat trap; usually some mechanical heating system is required.

Q: *How much sunshine do you really get in winter?*

A: More than is generally believed. Following is the percentage of hours of sunshine in relation to the possible daylight hours for the period of September 15-June 15 in thirty-three widely scattered cities, based on weather-bureau records averaging more than thirty years:

	Length of weather records	Percentage of sunshine hours
Atlanta	46 years	59.7
Boston	37	55
Chicago	39	53.6
Cincinnati	37	53
Columbus, Ohio	37	49.3
Dallas	30	59
Denver	40	66
Des Moines	37	57.3
Detroit	40	43.3
Galveston	53	60.4
Helena, Mont.	37	53
Houston	34	54
Indianapolis	34	52
Kansas City, Mo.	40	60.3
Little Rock	50	57
Los Angeles	47	72
Memphis	42	56
Milwaukee	30	52.6
Minneapolis	16	51
Montgomery, Ala.	33	62
New Orleans	53	56
New York City	36	58
Oklahoma City	46	63
Philadelphia	50	57.3
Pittsburgh	34	46.6
Portland, Ore.	53	38.8
Salt Lake City	41	62
San Antonio	38	55
San Francisco	53	66
Seattle	48	39.3
Spokane	46	46.5
Tampa	47	65.44
Toledo	31	46.3

Q: *What kind of artificial lighting should a solar house have?*

A: Here again is a question to be worked out in consultation with your architect.

Q: *Do you get a sunburn in a solar house?*

A: No. Ultraviolet rays, which cause sunburn, do not filter through glass used in houses. The rays which penetrate glass are infrared rays, which provide radiant-heat energy.

Q: *Do big windows cause glare?*

A: On the contrary, they reduce glare by eliminating sharp contrasts of light and dark. Reflective objects on the outside will throw a glare even through the smallest windows and should be avoided in planning the relationship of your solar house to exterior factors.

Q: *Can you cut off the daylight in a solar house?*

A: Easily. It is controlled by drapes, Venetian blinds, screens, or other shading devices.

Q: *How much additional daylight can I get into a house by using larger windows?*

A: That depends, of course, upon the dimensional expanse of the window area. However, in a "daylight engineering" test of a solar-house living room, lighting experts made an interesting discovery. Using a light meter, they found that there were 39 foot-candles of light in the middle of the room. (The test was made about 11 A.M. on an average day.) Then a previously prepared "mask" was put in place along the window wall. It contained three windows, transforming the wall into an ordinary type of living-room wall. The operation took five minutes and ten seconds. The next light-meter reading showed only 9 foot-candles, a loss of 30 foot-candles of natural light.

Q: *What about cleaning all those big windows?*

A: Big windows, or glass walls, have no muntins, or crossbars, and are easy to clean. They present fewer corners, usually the most difficult part of the window to clean.

Q: *Is it hard to keep a solar house clean?*

A: Not at all. Large windows admit daylight generously to far corners and make it easier for the housewife to see when she cleans. The fact that the south wall is largely of glass and that other windows are generally large means there will be less wallpaper to clean, less wall surface to wash. As for cleaning the window wall itself, it is easy to do with a squeegee.

Q: *How must I furnish a solar house?*

A: You may furnish it in any period or style you find suitable to the atmosphere it provides. Obviously you would not want to burden a light, airy interior with heavy ornamentation and dark, heavy trappings.

Q: *What kinds of draperies are used in solar houses?*

A: As for style, materials, and colors, the occupants' own decorative tastes dictate. But most solar-house dwellers choose a material that is translucent in order to admit light in plenty, but not transparent enough to threaten privacy when it is desired. Drapes usually should be large enough to be drawn across the entire south window wall at times for the sake of privacy. For this reason drapery materials should not be too heavy or bulky.

Q: *How can I enhance the night view from my solar windows?*

A: You may use floodlights, concealed in trees or shrubbery, to illuminate your garden in summer. In winter their beams will trap the blizzard's snow-filled gusts in a dramatic spectacle.

Q: *The view of the outdoors may be beautiful part of the year, but isn't it bleak in winter?*

A: It needn't be. Attractive landscaping with generous use and thoughtful placing of evergreens, trees and shrubs, assures an outdoor vista of something green the year around. The planning of a garden for new flowers and shrubs that come into bloom successively as their natural flowering periods follow, one upon the other, provides for the dweller in the solar house a spectacle of ever-changing nature.

Q: *Do plants grow well in a solar house?*

A: Luxuriantly and hardily. And they are an integral part of design in modern architecture. They are living adornments, giving vitality, variety, and continual change to interiors.

Q: *Is a solar house a "glass house"?*

A: No. Far from it. The opening of one wall through large windows does not displace the masonry and conventional windows of which the other three walls are formed. A solar house is merely a dwelling with the south wall providing large glass areas through which to admit the cheerful light of the sun and to join the sense of out-of-doors with the interior.

Q: *Are there any advantages to solar housing other than the gain of heat from the sun?*

A: The intellectual, emotional, and aesthetic gains, the increased livability, the satisfaction afforded by wedding exteriors and interiors in a single experience, are clearly as solid as the economic gain.

Q: *Should kitchens have large windows?*

A: Sunlight and a view will certainly provide a happier working atmosphere for those charged with the duties of operating a house. If a kitchen window overlooks a play area it affords easy opportunity for keeping track of the children.

Q: *What is a picture window?*

A: It is a large window opening glazed with an uninterrupted expanse of glass, that is, with no muntins, as in the case of the same opening glazed with many panes of glass. The view is not broken up. In effect, the exterior scene is framed as a living mural—thus the expression, picture window.

Q: *Will my solar-house windows frost up in winter?*

A: In solar houses with windows which are permanently double-glazed, with a sealed, dehydrated, insulating air space between the panes, frost will not form except under extreme conditions, such as sub-zero weather combined with excessive interior humidity.

Q: *Is a solar farmhouse practical?*

A: Yes. Actually, the location of the average farm dwelling is such that solar-type architecture is ideal. Completely rural surroundings offer a fine setting for a solar house.

Q: *Can solar architecture be adapted to an apartment building?*

A: Yes. The first step in that direction is, of course, the two-story house. There is no reason why, through proper design, the idea cannot be carried upward in multi-storied construction—just as it has been and is being done in many new hospitals and other public buildings.

Q: *Can I replace my present windows with permanent double-glazing?*

A: Yes, but it is not always economical. Storm sash may be added easily to single-glazed windows, but in the case of replacement with permanent double-glazed panes, the wider sash often required to accommodate the two panes of glass and the air space between them necessitates construction that might not justify the extra cost. Get an estimate before ordering such replacements. In new construction, the cost factors are different.

Q: *Can I convert my present dwelling to a solar house?*

A: Usually it is expensive and difficult. Old dwellings have been converted to solar houses, so it can be done if conditions are right. Better consult your architect.

Q: *Is a solar house a new idea, a fad?*

A: It certainly is not. The principle of opening a house to the south to admit the low sun in winter and to shut it out in summertime is thousands of years old. Xenophon wrote about it in the third century before the time of Christ.

Q: *Who invented the solar house?*

A: The solar house is not an "invention." It is an evolution of architectural form which has taken place over thousands of years.

Familiar type of window. Note how the horizontal and vertical muntins, or cross-bars, divide the glass into many small panes, interfere with good vision and present an annoying barrier to full enjoyment of the view.

A step toward better vision. This windowpane is in keeping with modern trends. All vertical muntins have been removed. Incidentally, such a window offers more economies in repainting or cleaning.

Note how the same view improves when seen through this large modern-type of windowpane—a "picture window." Any beautiful bits of scenery—a lawn, garden, or trees—changing with the seasons become a year-around mural.

49

SOLAR HOUSES

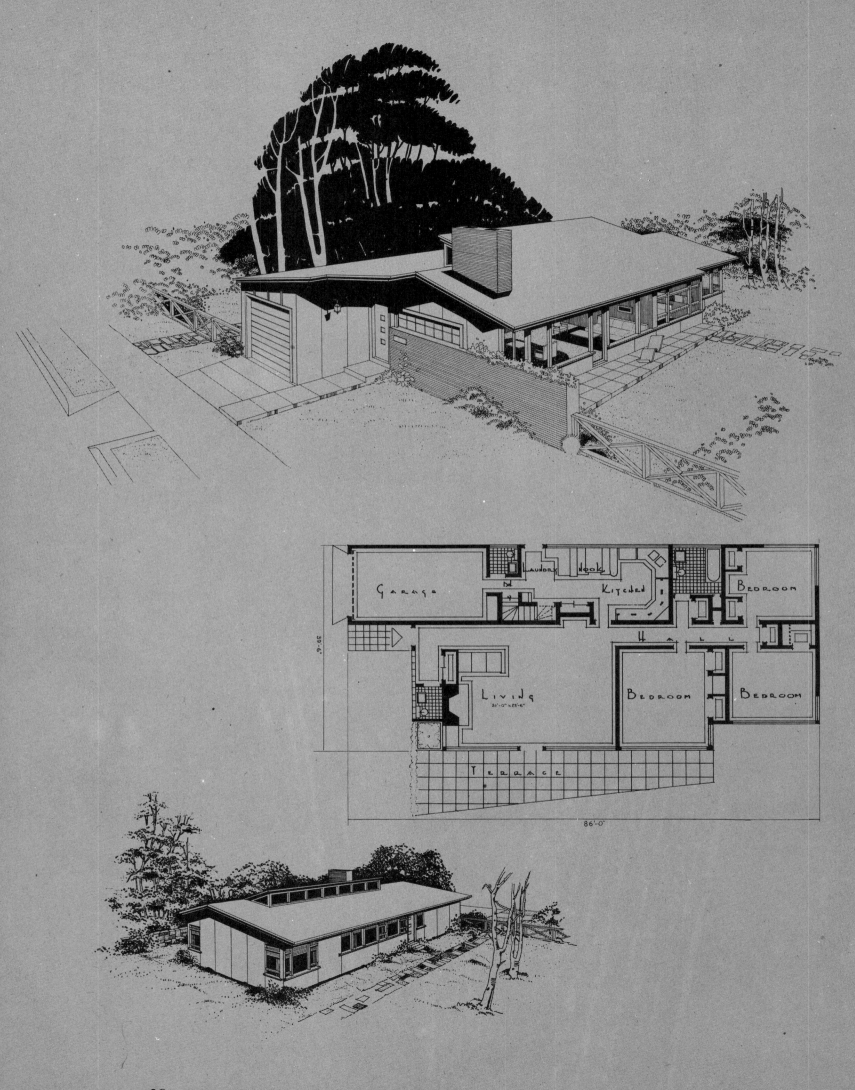

Garage

Laundry Nook

Kitchen

Bedroom

39'-6"

Living
31'-0" x 23'-6"

Hall

Bedroom

Bedroom

Terrace

86'-0"

28

MAINE

AMBROSE S. HIGGINS
Architect

In Maine most housing problems normally revolve about our chief topic of conversation, the weather. Our state is known extensively as a vacation state, but living in Maine throughout the year requires a lot of thinking about the nine months little known to the summer rusticator.

The winters are long and their days are short. Any sunny period is welcome in this long, cold season. A solar house, therefore, has unique appeal here both from psychological and from economic viewpoints.

We will set our house back toward the north line of our lot, giving us the full use of the land for landscaping, gardening, and the developing of an estate appearance.

Our house will have large glass areas facing south, especially useful in Maine. Thermopane fulfills the ordinary need, extraordinarily realized, of a window. Moreover, carrying its own insulation, it performs the function of the storm window. The Thermopane admits the radiant heat of the sun and traps it within the house. It also serves to keep the heat from the central system within the house. No Yankee will argue the value of conserving heat supplied by sun and fuel.

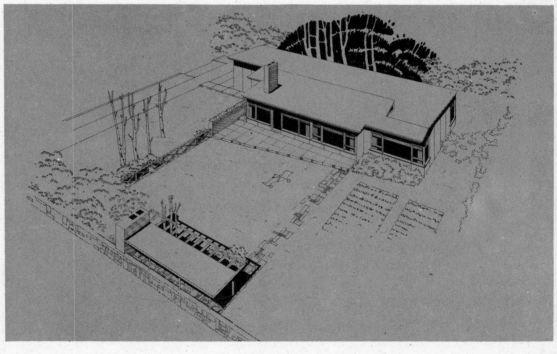

Nor will his wife overlook the psychological value of admitting more light in our dark winters. She will be cheered by the gayer atmosphere, the more open feeling given to the north wall of her living room by clerestory windows.

Her husband also will be pleased that most of the structural materials are products of the state of Maine. The native white-pine exterior, the molded battens, the stone, brick, and even the cement are all indigenous. He knows just what are the possibilities and limitations of these products. He also knows that a low building makes for low heating costs, and that the elimination of angles results in compactness of plan.

The summer and early fall are not forgotten in planning the house. Occasionally the temperature rises to 100 degrees plus. The blueberry and other crops have been lost in drought years.

The roof overhang is designed to minimize the heat of the sun's rays.

The interior, no less than the exterior, combines consideration of climate and general livability. A sociologist once said that architects designed houses as if they never heard of children. This house is designed with father, mother, and at least two children in mind. All of them, again, living in Maine.

The children in this house will come home at noon, hang their winter clothes in a closet built in as part of the utility space, wash up in a lavatory near the entrance, have their lunch, and return to school; so, too, the husband, who comes home for the midday meal, as do many down-Mainers. In inclement weather, the youngsters may play in the basement room that houses the compact heating unit.

Visiting is still a cherished custom in Maine. A front entrance is designed for convenience of visitors. A guest may enter, hang his heavy outer garment in a closet, then enter the living room directly without tracking in the snow of winter or the mud of spring. This house, then, has been designed to achieve the maximum for an investment in a home built in Maine.

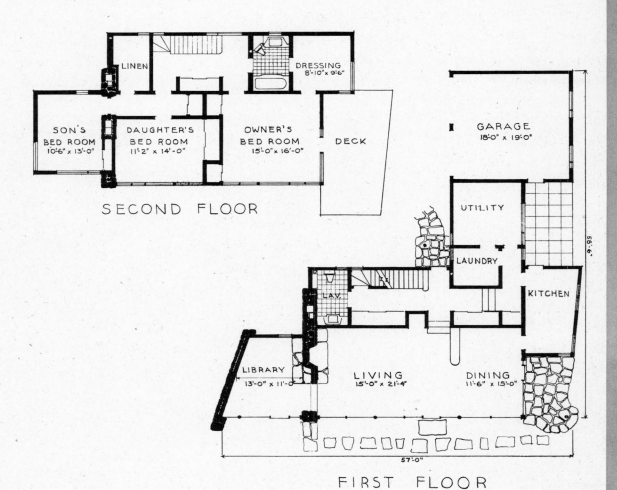

LINEN

DRESSING
8'-10" x 9'-6"

SON'S
BED ROOM
10'-6" x 13'-0"

DAUGHTER'S
BED ROOM
11'-2" x 14'-0"

OWNER'S
BED ROOM
15'-0" x 16'-0"

DECK

GARAGE
18'-0" x 19'-0"

SECOND FLOOR

UTILITY

LAUNDRY

KITCHEN

LAV.

LIBRARY
13'-0" x 11'-0"

LIVING
15'-0" x 21'-4"

DINING
11'-6" x 15'-0"

55'-9"

57'-0"

FIRST FLOOR

NEW HAMPSHIRE

JOHN F. G. GUNTHER
*Architect**

NEW HAMPSHIRE is a land of cool summer holidays and rugged winter sport. But whether you are a native or a visitor—following a mountain trail in August, or schussing a ski run in January—you probably think of a New Hampshire winter as traditionally given over to stoking the furnace and shutting out the snow and cold.

Modern house design makes this no longer necessary. The solar house provides comfort and protection in the coldest weather, with less artificial heating than the traditional New England farmhouse of comparable living space requires. The generous expanse of glass, in conjunction with projecting roofs on the southern side, serves a multiple purpose.

Through the large windows the beauty of the snow-clad hills merges with the interior of the rooms, and the low winter sun gives more gracious and more economical warmth than the conventional heating plant. The house, filled with sunlight which supplements the artificial heat, will be bright and cheerful. The winter will lose its forbidding face and assume an aspect of charm and beauty.

The double glass of Thermopane now offers to the New Hampshire house the advantages of large windows which need no storm sash.

With complete protection from the weather, the occupants, gathered in warmth about the fireplace of library or living room, may sit and enjoy, untroubled, the snow-filled gusts of a New England blizzard.

In its detail treatment, the house blends the rugged simplicity of its New Hampshire setting with the most modern appointments. The exterior is finished in the

traditional New England clapboard with an admixture of vertical boarding and battens to create a contrast of textures. The massive field-stone chimney and library wall, exposed on the interior as well as on the outside, are indigenous to the rocky terrain of the state.

In general form, the exterior mass accentuates the horizontal, to present an interesting relationship with the mountainous character of the region. It is perfectly practical to build the specified roof with ample capacity

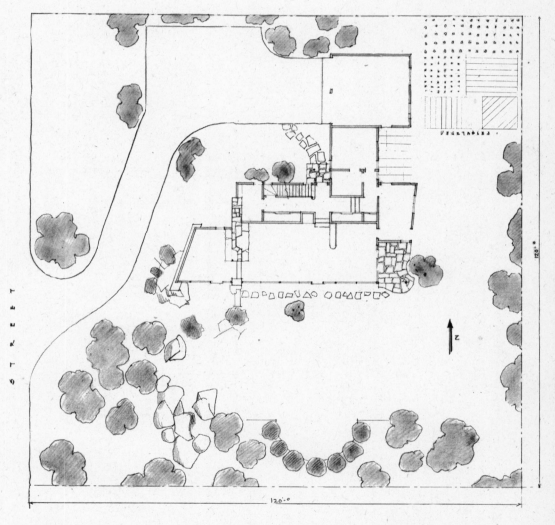

for heavy snow loads, and with modern materials and techniques and proper insulation this construction will probably cost less than the typical sloping roof.

The entire house has been conceived to supply the aesthetic and practical requirements for gracious living. It is intended to furnish shelter as such, to a degree which only modern materials and equipment can provide, and to create an ideal atmosphere and environment as well. *Mr. Gunther died shortly after completion of his solar house design. Final work was carried on by Phillip H. Rogers, Architect.

play area

service

kitchen

dining~living
20'-0" x 14'-0"

terrace

grille

chute

laundry

study~guest

garage

to basement

n

living floor

34'-4"

11'-8"

26'-8"

17'-4"

12'-4"

boy

girl

owner

chute

bath

dressing

22'-0"

sleeping floor

VERMONT

RUTH REYNOLDS FREEMAN
Architect

THE NATIVE VERMONTER is inherently conservative. He accepts new materials and new theories only after they have been tested or when they appeal definitely to his pocketbook. When he applies these characteristics to house building, they result in a home of sound construction, with the choice of materials carefully balanced in relation to the over-all budget as well as to their use in relation to other materials.

Vermont's people are acutely aware of the extreme weather conditions in their state. The stories of temperatures 35 or 45 below zero are not fiction but bitter fact which, although not common, the Vermonter nevertheless must face and overcome if he wishes to build a home that will assure him of comfort throughout the long, cold winter.

The accepted frost line throughout Vermont is five feet. The cost of excavating for foundations to this depth is such that the cost of a complete cellar is very little more and gives the house assurance of a warm floor as well as necessary storage space and work space. The basement has been left open with no finish, to allow future development as time may indicate, and to avoid additional expense at the time of initial construction.

A full basement under the main mass of the house provides an easy means of installing a heating system. Our experience indicates that the most satisfactory system for Vermont homes is one which allows rapid changes in temperature when required to match extreme changes in the weather, and provides a simple means of removing the chill from the house in spring and fall, an essential correction in this climate. It is also a most satisfactory adjunct of solar design, making possible the maintenance of a comfortable temperature throughout the house during early winter mornings, with the heating plant shutting down completely in the hours when the sun will pour through the large Thermopane areas. The resulting saving in the fuel bill will please the owner's pocketbook.

The room arrangement has been developed carefully to take full advantage of the maximum possible solar energy during the winter months, and to assure a minimum of heat penetration in the summertime. The glass areas throughout are of Thermopane, and ventilation is accomplished by use of standard double-hung windows common throughout Vermont and readily

available. The garage has been placed on the front of the house, projecting forward to the street, to assure a minimum of driveway from which snow has to be removed. The garage and a multi-purpose room protect the front doorway from severe snowdrifting.

The exterior seeks to express the inherent qualities of simplicity and of blending with the countryside typical of the two-story Vermont farmhouse. An exterior of barn red with off-white trim is planned. The roof was first considered to be a straight pitch with overhang at the south for solar control. After considerable thought we agreed that this would be too extreme and not acceptable to the average Vermonter, even though he might have strong tendencies toward the modern in design. Actually, the roof shown would be of more economical construction and would assure a minimum of snow accumulation as well as drainage without complicated gutters or leaders which are so often subject to freezing.

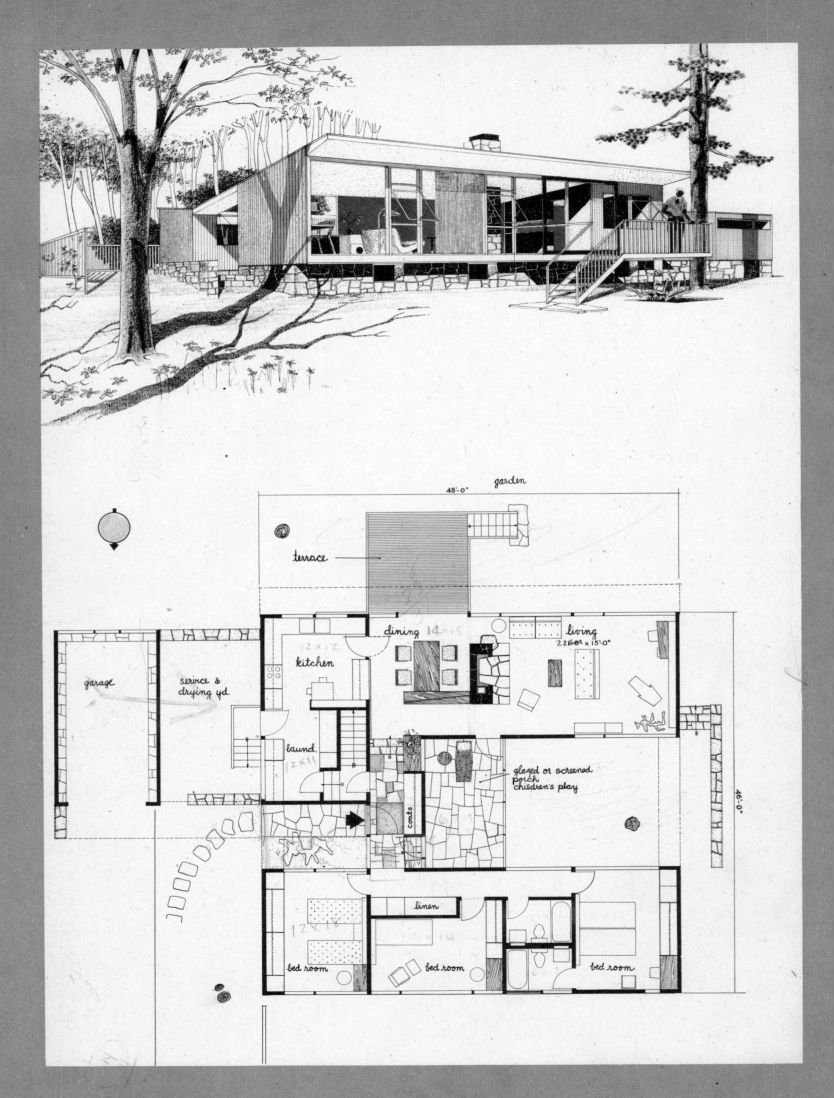

garden

48'-0"

terrace

dining 14 x 15

living
22'-8" x 15'-0"

kitchen
12 x 12

garage

service & drying yd.

laund.
12 x 11

coats

glazed or screened porch
children's play

46'-0"

linen

bed room
12 x 18

bed room

bed room

34

MASSACHUSETTS

HUGH STUBBINS, JR.
Architect

THE PLAN of this house had to solve two separate problems and to reconcile each one to the other.

The first, which always exists in the design of a house, is how to plan it for livability, utility, and charm. Livability and charm in many respects are closely linked. Utility is a matter of good equipment, good and sensible materials and construction, and proper arrangement.

The second problem reposed in the fact that the house was to be designed neither for a specific site nor for a specific family. Thus, to my mind, it became mandatory that the basic design be as flexible as possible, flexible enough to fit any orientation and to fit a reasonable slope in either direction or even a piece of level ground. An absolutely level piece of land is found but rarely in Massachusetts, and some land suitable for building sites is fairly rocky, or even ledgy.

Design in the light of the first problem is based primarily on the separation of facilities for eating, playing, and relaxing from the accommodations for dressing and sleeping. In this case the separation was accomplished by making two rectangular wings, spaced apart and connected by a covered link which is in fact the entrance to the house. These two wings and their connecting link form a small, intimate garden court onto which the living room opens.

In the New England climate a small, protected outdoor court is a welcome feature in early spring and late fall and, since the living room opens onto this as well as onto a larger garden in the rear of the lot, it provides a choice of an outdoor annex.

Further to utilize the space between the wings, a covered porch parallels the entrance link (or hall) and may be screened in summer or glassed in for winter. This really is a multi-purpose room which may be used for hobbies and recreation.

The placing of the living-dining area and the kitchen in one wing and the bedrooms and baths in another also meets the considerations of flexibility, unspecified plot, and unforeseen orientation. Major openings may be placed on either side, dictated only by orientation, which is important not only in a solar house but in any house. By having the link between the two main elements and a loosely attached garage, it is easy to adjust the design to a sloping lot by introducing steps in the link, thus accommodating the difference in grade.

In this plan the sleeping wing always protects the living-room wing from the street, regardless of orientation, and is in turn protected by a setback and by screening with a louvered fence or planting. No windows open on the sides of the house, thus giving privacy from adjacent lots.

As the design is presented, the street is assumed to be on the north side of a site which slopes downward toward the south. Each room has southern sunlight and cross-ventilation. By slight elevation of the living-room wing a basement under this portion is obtained without excavation. If on level, rocky ground, where a basement is undesirable, the heater room takes the space occupied by the basement stair.

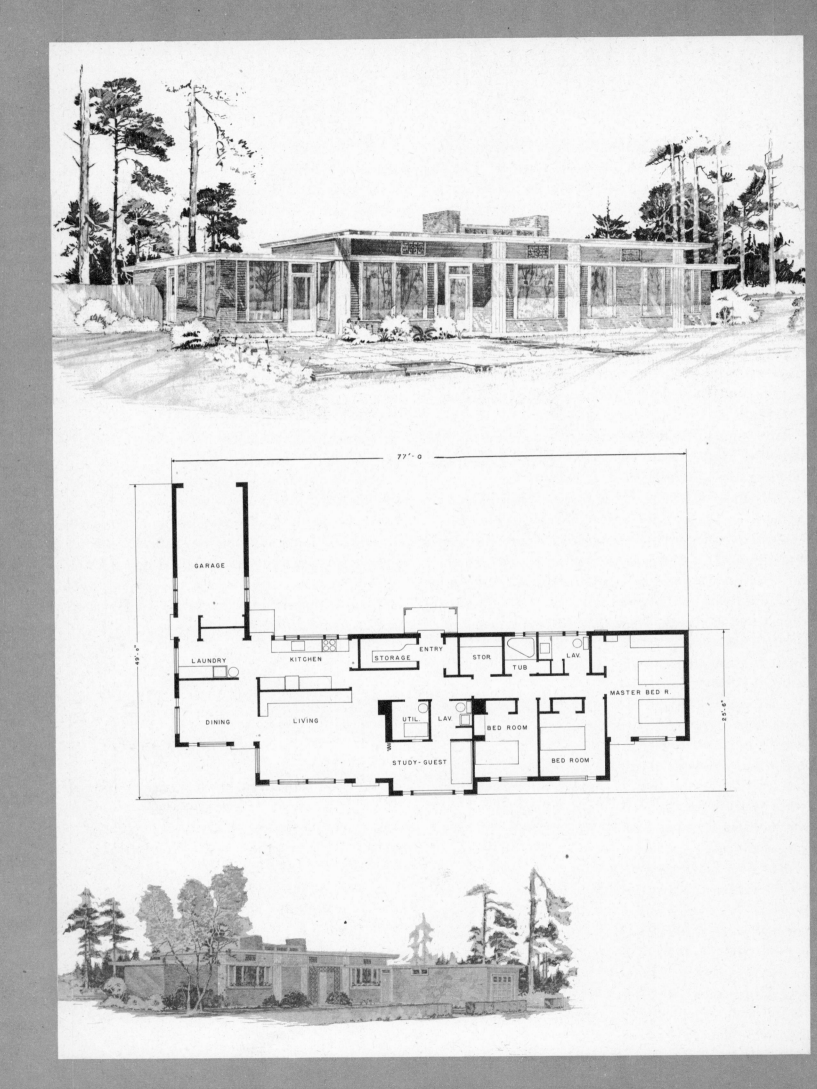

GARAGE

LAUNDRY

KITCHEN

STORAGE

ENTRY

STOR.

TUB

LAV.

DINING

LIVING

UTIL.

LAV.

BED ROOM

MASTER BED R.

STUDY-GUEST

BED ROOM

77'-0

49'-0"

25'-6"

CONNECTICUT

DOUGLAS ORR
Architect

THE GENERAL CONCEPT of this design is based on efficient planning, ease of household care, pleasant living, and something of the feeling of earlier Connecticut houses. Much consideration has been given to storage requirements and the proper placing of the units.

Because of the fitness of the small Greek-revival house so familiar in Connecticut, this *general* feeling is reflected in the solar house. While *no* attempt has been made to design the building as Greek revival, that spirit is characteristic of Connecticut in its simplicity and dignity.

The house is designed to be built of frame with brick veneer, with flush boarding in the frieze penetrated by the cast-iron grilles. It was planned in a symmetrical manner, with the main entrance provided with a covered porch on the north side. The desirability of an entrance porch in Connecticut continues, at least for our winter weather. The entrance hall has purposely not been carried directly into the main part of the living room making it possible, if desired, to introduce a second door at the back of the entry.

Adjacent to the entry is a storage space sufficiently ample to house such things as a perambulator and outdoor equipment which normally would not be put in the clothes closet on the opposite side.

Another ample storage space is provided in the bedroom hallway to take care of the numerous items required of a family living in a one-story house with neither attic nor basement storage space.

In the center of the house, adjacent to the utility room, is a lavatory which may serve either casual visitors or an overnight guest quartered in the combined study and guest room.

The living room contains a built-in desk with storage wall. The separated dining area may be used directly in conjunction with the living room by shortening the built-in storage wall or may be used independently. In either case the service from the kitchen is direct and simple.

Access from the drying yard or the garage is through the doorway to the west. This would serve as an entrance for children's bicycles or for garden equipment and tools.

Over the center area, which includes the heater room and lavatory, it is planned to develop a monitor, or raised section of the roof. This monitor is fitted with louvers and cast-iron grilles, providing ventilation for the heater room and lavatory. A ventilating fan placed in this raised portion serves to clear the air from the entire house and combat the humidity in the hot months.

The kitchen has been planned for a mechanical exhaust system over the fixtures, which exhausts through the grille in the frieze.

The other frieze grilles in the house are intended for summer circulation of air out of the top of the rooms, and the entrance of air in all cases through louvers on each side of the windows.

RHODE ISLAND

ALBERT HARKNESS
Architect

RHODE ISLAND, the most concentrated state in the union, with its vigorous changes in climate and its comparatively flat, unspectacular terrain, presents special requirements which lead this design into a distinctive trend.

Restriction of space and economy of heating result in this compact, two-story solution. The placing of the living room on the second floor provides a quiet, restful room and a feeling of spaciousness for the whole house, which otherwise would suffer from the compactness of the plan.

The second-floor location of the living room separates it from the general turmoil usually present in even the quietest family existence. Placed at the head of the stairs, it is entirely shut off even from the sleeping area. At the same time the living room and porch get a better view, a breeze, and a feeling of grandeur not expected in so small a house.

All the principal activities associated with the management and operation of a home are centered on the first floor.

From the kitchen-laundry there are supervision of the garden, direct contact with the dining area, and observation of the play area when the folding partitions are open. The play area is for the various hobbies of occupants of all ages, thus keeping the living room free of the clutter usually attending such activities. The barbecue area on the first floor also is a noteworthy feature.

The modern automobile, with its wide doors, creates a problem in a one-car garage. The solution has been found by planning a loading platform at the side of the garage, one step up from the floor.

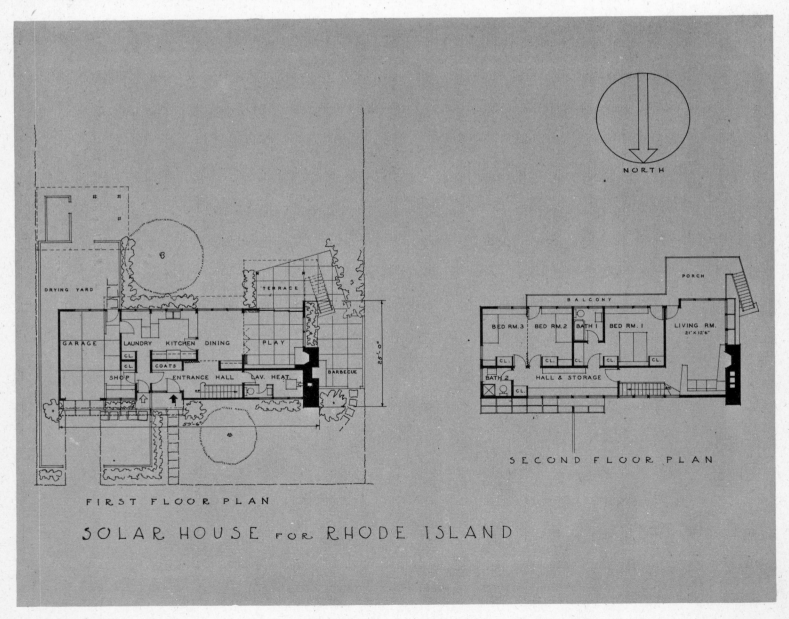

FIRST FLOOR PLAN

SECOND FLOOR PLAN

SOLAR HOUSE FOR RHODE ISLAND

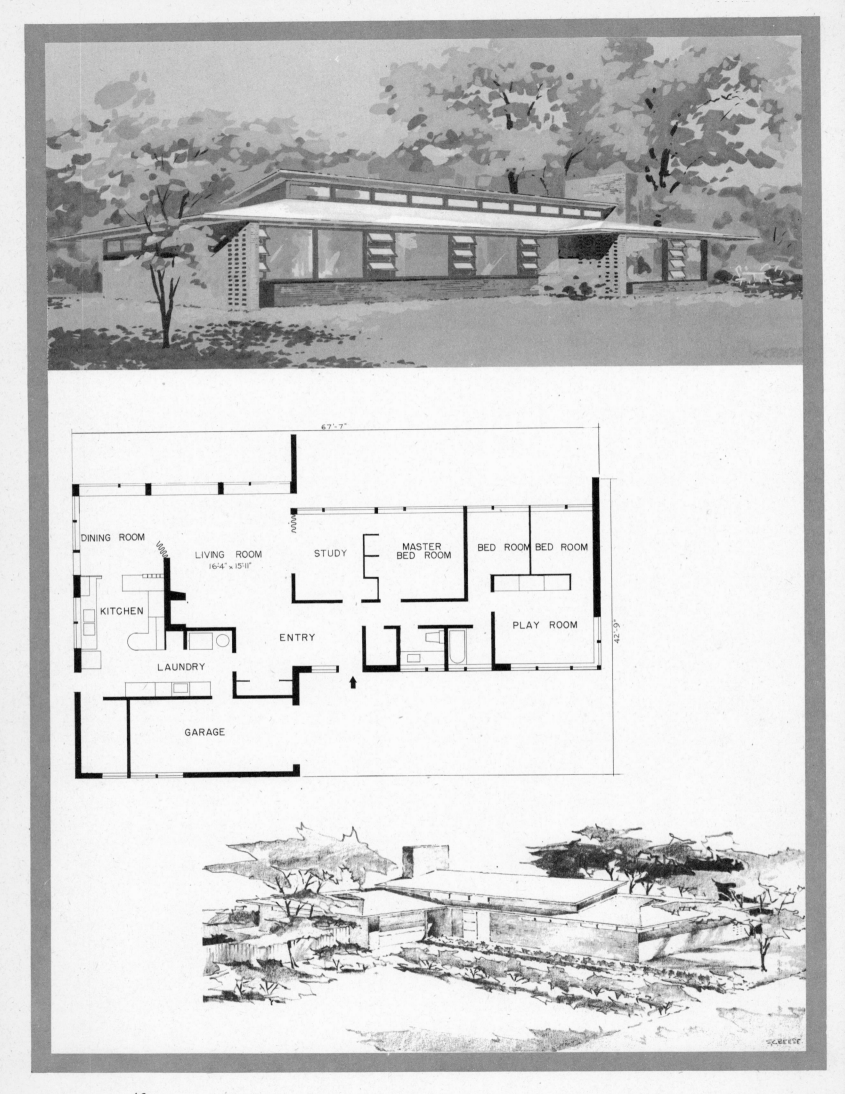

DINING ROOM

67'-7"

KITCHEN

LIVING ROOM
16'-4" x 15'-11"

STUDY

MASTER
BED ROOM

BED ROOM BED ROOM

PLAY ROOM

ENTRY

LAUNDRY

42'-9"

GARAGE

40

NEW YORK

EDWARD D. STONE
Architect

SEVERAL CIRCUMSTANCES peculiar to New York State and the life of its inhabitants influenced this design. The extremely high cost of land necessitated a scheme which makes maximum use of the plot. Extremes of weather require that the house be easily heated, and that it take every possible advantage of solar radiation. The cosmopolitan tastes of New Yorkers, their gregarious social habits, and their streamlined existence make it mandatory that the aesthetic appeal of the house be universal, and that it be an economic plan with ample facilities for entertainment.

We assumed a building site with a street on the west side, and placed the house as close as possible to the north property line. With the *front* yard thus minimized and the house approached along the north side, a large proportion of the lot remains useful as a sunny private garden, the other with the living-dining area.

All major rooms have full southern exposure, and the dining area has south and east exposure. Because of the difficulties involved in controlling sunlight from the west, most of the street side is windowless.

The house is divided into a work area, a dining and living area, and a bedroom area. All three are adjacent to the entry, with resulting isolation of the living and dining rooms so that these may be private for adult entertainment.

The kitchen is generous in size and has a counter for breakfast or for children's dining. Near the back door of the house is ample space for storing outdoor furniture, trunks, sports equipment, and gardening tools. Its proximity to the kitchen makes it convenient for food storage as well.

The large brick extension of the hearth is a feature of the living room. Fireplace and glass wall are at right angles to each other, so that either may be the center of

attraction without changing furniture arrangement.

A small study adjacent to the living room serves not only as a quiet retreat, a children's study, or a guest room, but also may function in conjunction with the master bedroom to provide a two-room suite for the parents. It is separated from the living room or made a part of it by use of a folding partition.

The children's bedrooms are small. They have a playroom, which in later years may serve as a large bedroom while their two former rooms may be converted into a second by removal of the partition that divides them.

The highly desirable southern exposure has been allotted to principal rooms. The kitchen and dining alcove enjoy eastern exposure for sunny breakfasting. South light is further introduced into entry, bath, and playrooms by means of a strip of clerestory windows in the roof. This permits the use of an extremely large area of glass facing the southern sun without resorting to high eaves or to extreme attenuation of plan.

It was of prime concern to the architect to produce a house with all conceivable solar advantages which would still be harmonious with conservative tastes. Low-pitched roofs and long overhangs increase the feeling of shelter, while the use of unpainted brick and stained wood blends well with existing houses and with the New York landscape.

PENNSYLVANIA

OSCAR STONOROV and LOUIS I. KAHN
Architects

FINE eighteenth-century farmhouses of stone, the nineteenth-century colonial manors of brick, and the informally eclectic English suburban houses of the early years of the present century attest Pennsylvania's long tradition in home architecture. A contemporary approach to living is decidedly within this tradition.

The modern structure, so called, may be as much a part of the Pennsylvania landscape as the old houses. Wood, glass, stone or brick, whitewashed or not, are natural elements. With the availability of glass in large sheets and the desirability of using it for handsome vistas or for sun heating, a formula for a Pennsylvania solar house is arrived at easily.

The modified square shape, with the east and west sides favoring the south, offers, by analysis, greater solar advantages than the formal square. The full south wall and about half of the east and west walls are opened to the sun—protected from it, as they should be, in summer, and inviting its pleasant, warming rays in winter. The north wall is opened only for the house entrance and the bathroom windows on the second floor. Rooms are arranged along east-south and west exposures. The core of the plan contains heater, storage, stair, corridors, and bathrooms.

The masonry walls of the heater-storage area with their extensions bring about a positive division of the spaces. All other walls except the exterior ones are incidental and could be left out without harming the house. This makes for a sort of building procedure in stages, allowing the budget to keep up with the dreams.

In the plot plan shown here, the house is placed as close to the road as the garage permits. This is no detriment to livability; on the contrary, since the north wall acts as a barrier, the maximum garden area becomes available to the living room and terrace.

For this house the architect invented a client who is a composite of many clients: head of a family consisting of himself, a wife, and two children. This client readily accepts a logical approach to the problem of building; he does not becloud his needs and preferences with some preconceived notions of symmetry or roof. He appreciates that a house does not end with the walls which enclose it. He considers outdoor living space, play space, quiet areas, drying yard, sandbox, lawn, and garden all part of the general plan. He is conscious that the smaller the house, the more house and ground must become one—a home.

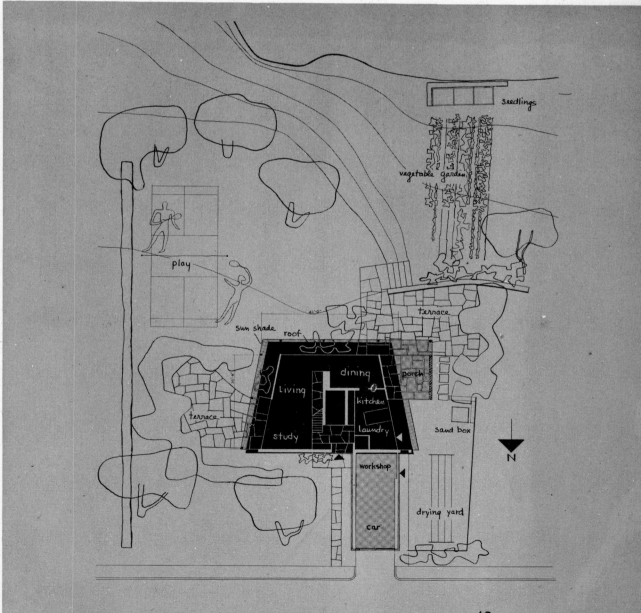

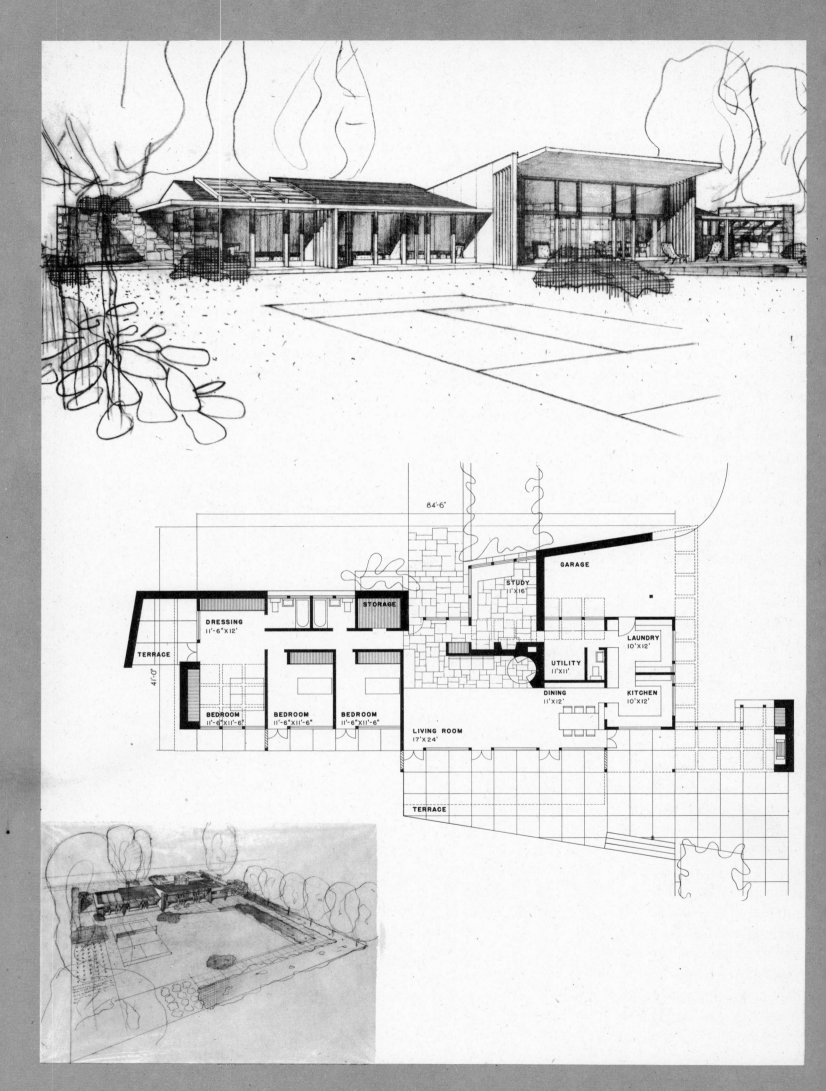

DRESSING
11'-6"x12'

STORAGE

TERRACE

41'-0"

BEDROOM
11'-6"x11'-6"

BEDROOM
11'-6"x11'-6"

BEDROOM
11'-6"x11'-6"

LIVING ROOM
17'x24'

84'-6"

GARAGE

STUDY
11'x16'

LAUNDRY
10'x12'

UTILITY
11'x11'

DINING
11'x12'

KITCHEN
10'x12'

TERRACE

NEW JERSEY

ALLMON FORDYCE
Architect

THIS HOUSE has been designed for persons who like to live in the sun and air, whose house and yard work together for their comfort and their recreation.

The design follows some of the traditions to which New Jersey's early settlers adhered in building their homes. Those old farmhouses usually were located on the protected southern slopes of the hills. The farmers faced their principal rooms toward the south to obtain the maximum warmth of the winter sun. Many of the houses had overhangs and porches on the southern exposure, to act as summer sunshades. Native fieldstone was used extensively for the houses, giving them an air of great solidity and protection from the elements, a heritage from the English and the Dutch who settled here.

The feeling of security achieved in those homes by the use of stone masonry and orientation to the sun has been utilized in this design by making the exposed north, east, and west walls of stone and the south front a screen of glass opening the house toward the garden and play areas.

The functions of the house may be divided into the family living space, a work space, and sleeping quarters. These functions of the New Jersey solar house are placed on one floor for convenience and minimum maintenance. The ground-floor slab acts as both foundation and heating element.

The family living space is entered through a translucent glass screen protected by the overhanging roof of the porch. The wide hall becomes part of the living room. The flagstone floor of the porch continues through the hall and merges with the hearth of the fireplace. The living and dining spaces work together as one room most of the time. A folding screen separates the dining space on formal occasions. The long side of this room is a glass screen facing south. A smaller room, off the hall, is used as a study and provides a quiet re-

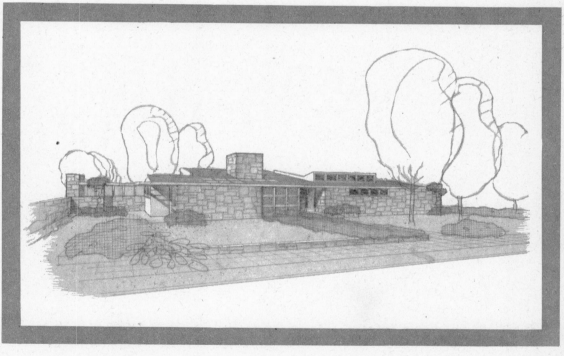

treat when the living room is being used for entertainment.

In the work space the kitchen, laundry, shop, heating element, and storage closets are arranged for convenience and to save steps and time. The facilities usually in the basement are brought upstairs into the light and air. The kitchen is placed for easy line production to the dining table and is conveniently located to the dining terrace and outdoor grill. The laundry-sewing room is convenient both to the kitchen work area and the service yard.

The sleeping quarters are in a wing separated from the other activities of the house. The bedroom hall is lighted and ventilated by a continuous dormer window at the ceiling. Opening off this hall is a walk-in seasonal storage closet. The two bedrooms for the children open on the south to the garden play areas, enabling them to play indoors in bad weather without a feeling of being shut in. Their two rooms may be thrown together by making the separating wall a folding partition. The master bedroom is divided into dressing space and sleeping space by sliding glass doors. The sleeping space has a glass south wall and a glass ceiling which give it the effect of an outdoor room. Over the glass roof are adjustable louvers; closing them shades the area on hot days; opening them at night permits the occupants to sleep under the stars.

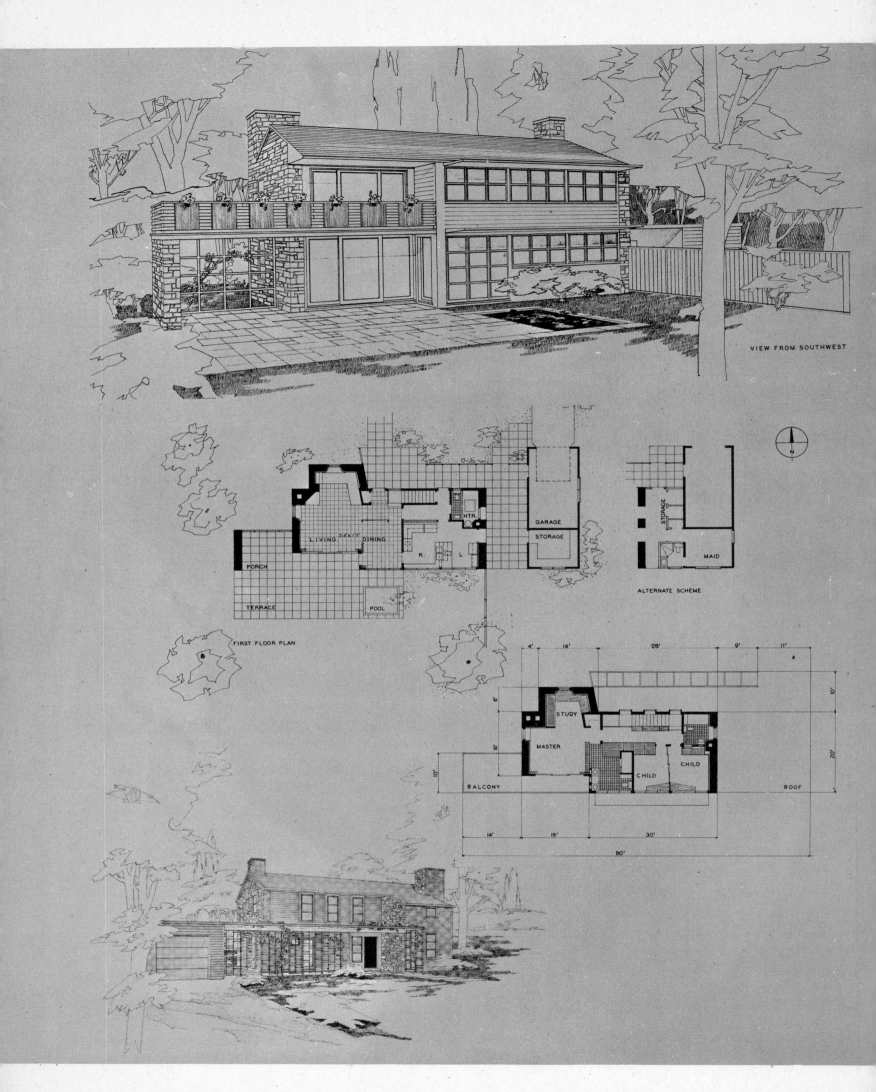

VIEW FROM SOUTHWEST

PORCH

LIVING 24'x17' DINING

HTR.

K. L

GARAGE

STORAGE

TERRACE

POOL

FIRST FLOOR PLAN

STORAGE

MAID

ALTERNATE SCHEME

N

4' 14' 28' 9' 11'

STUDY

MASTER

CHILD

CHILD

BALCONY

ROOF

10'

20'

10'

6'

16'

14' 16' 30'

80'

DELAWARE

VICTORINE and SAMUEL HOMSEY
Architects

IN DESIGNING a solar house for this state, we felt that the traditions of Delaware architecture should not be overlooked so long as they did not interfere with the livability which has become possible through the introduction of new materials and new structural practices. Thus we have analyzed what of the old is still solid practice for modern design and practical for modern structural methods.

ISOMETRIC OF PLOT ARRANGEMENT

The native stone is not only beautiful but comparatively inexpensive. There are workmen still to be found who understand how to construct a really fine wall. The only disadvantage of stone walls is the thickness, which takes from the size of the rooms, but here again we find old builders embracing the sensible solution of confining the masonry to the end walls where the chimneys are located, with stud walls on the long sides, allowing greater interior width without adding to the framing, especially the length of roof rafters.

In considering this, it was only a short step to the introduction of a glass wall on the long south side of this house, in place of the stud wall, and with careful study of eave and intermediate projections, a solar house appeared.

In the masonry walls, another typical Delaware fea-

ture is the rounded splays at the window jambs. This, of course, adds to the light without weakening the wall, and is a most attractive form. The typical pitched roof of Delaware also has advantages. The attic space, if well vented, allows for one or two exhaust fans which are essential for our long, hot summers.

The entrance on the north indicates its Delaware character in the use of masonry, siding, pitched roof, and irregular eave heights. The proportion of the windows is typical of Delaware, although they are not conventionally placed and have large panes of glass.

From the entrance of the house, the living and dining rooms, with glass walls on the south, present a spaciousness and adaptability which are not found in the traditional division of rooms. The informality and homelike feeling, however, are maintained by the irregular shape of the rooms, allowing a permanent sitting place looking toward the fire and a more open area where lighter furniture may be moved about at will.

On the second floor the master bedroom has its own balcony and dressing alcove with built-in cupboards, counters, and other fixtures. The children's rooms, while small, may be converted into one large room by sliding panels. The built-in furniture allows greater floor space for play.

The garden to the south is most important. We feel strongly that glass walls should never be used unless an enclosed garden is designed at the same time which not only gives privacy but has such interest in design and plant material as to make it attractive at all seasons, in whatever climate the house is built. This is absolutely essential in the city and important in the country, except when the house is built on a hill so that the south is open to a distant view while being entirely private.

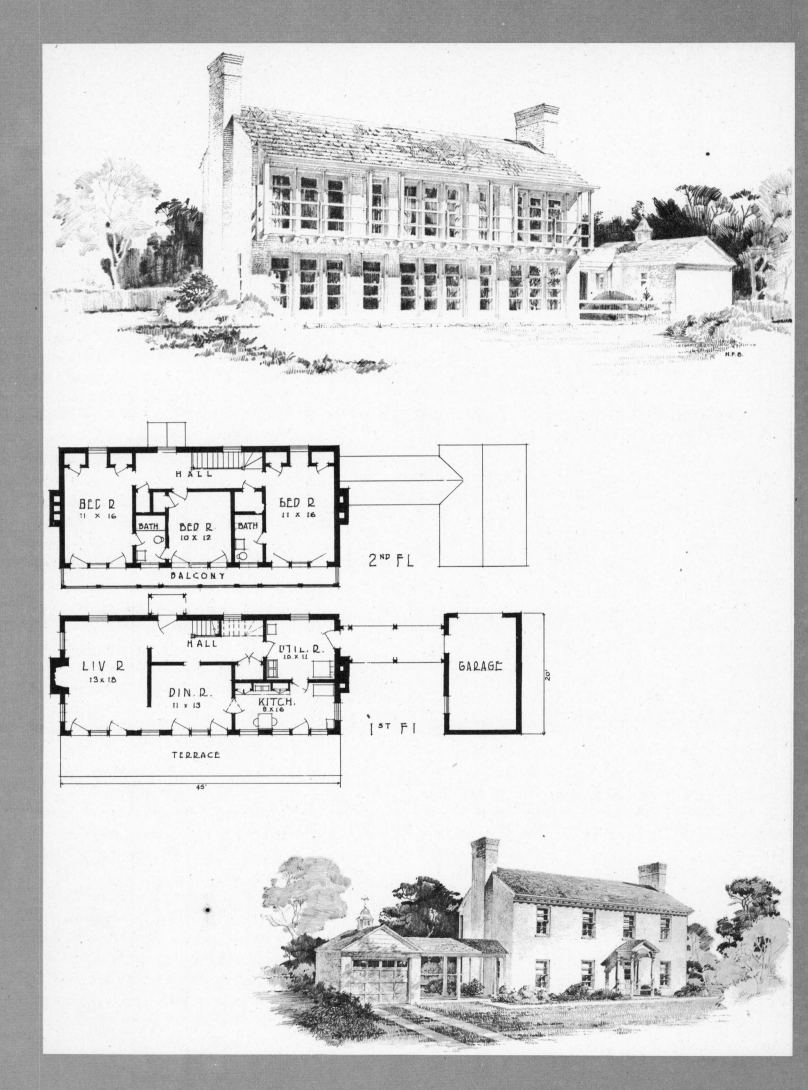

2ND FL

HALL

BED R
11 x 16

BATH

BED R
10 x 12

BATH

BED R
11 x 16

BALCONY

1ST FL

HALL

LIV R
13 x 18

DIN. R.
11 x 13

KITCH.
8 x 16

UTIL. R.
10 x 11

GARAGE

20'

TERRACE

45'

H.F.B.

MARYLAND

T. WORTH JAMISON, JR.
Architect

THE EARLY MARYLAND farmhouse pointed a solution for the design problem of the Maryland solar house. At first blush the use of glass to the extent necessary for solar heating and "solar living" seemed incompatible with the limitations of traditional design. A variant of the "one-room-thick" farmhouse, however, offered a solution since it permitted all the large openings required for adequate solar transmission to be restricted to the south side, leaving north, east, and west free for the characteristic expression of native taste, which demands large wall areas and windows of conventional proportion.

This avoidance of extreme character and retention of some indigenous feeling bid for approval in almost any suburban development, even the most restricted. The house is neither freakish nor bizarre.

The plans were kept simple and straightforward for ease of circulation and livability and also for simplicity of construction, which in turn makes for minimum cost.

Materials proposed for the structure are common brick for the exterior walls, painted white, or a hard-burned "colonial" type of brick, unpainted. The roof is gray or black slate, random in widths and fairly rough in texture. Terrace and walks are flagstone from local quarries.

The interior finish would be adaptable to individual taste. To enhance the apparent size of the living room, a large mirror, under which a large sofa may be placed, is indicated on the wall opposite the fireplace. The living room, dining room, and kitchen all will enjoy an abundance of sunshine in winter months, as will the bedrooms and baths. The large opening groups which make this possible will be provided with traverse curtains to temper the sunlight or to make for privacy after dark.

The balcony and its roof were designed to shield the southern openings in summer when the sun is to the north, at the same time adhering to traditional motives. Since the prevailing summer breezes are from the southwest, out-of-door shade is also achieved to the best advantage.

We believe that the house-conscious public in this state is sufficiently acquainted with traditional design and with modern trend to respond gratifyingly to the solution offered here.

49

DISTRICT OF COLUMBIA

ALFRED KASTNER
Architect

ARCHITECTURALLY speaking, this area is dominated by one structure: the Washington Monument. Its abstract and timeless beauty as an object by itself, its relation to other objects, and its evident success as a solution to functional, historical, and emotional aspects remains unchallenged.

At the monument's base there are magnificent parks bounded by wide, tree-bordered avenues. As these extend from the monument to undertake the prosaic function of serving a rapidly growing city of average metropolitan character, there remain everywhere the noble trees as the co-ordinating element of the Federal City.

In this setting the designing of a residence offers considerable latitude, particularly when the client's social ambitions afford him an independent outlook. If we assume this, and further that there is available a typical District of Columbia building lot of average dimensions facing north, basic orientation will require placing the service areas toward the street and the living areas toward the garden.

On a foundation of rough field-stone masonry, the superstructure sits as a clean-cut cube. The house is of two stories and basement. The first floor contains the living-dining areas, extending across the entire south face of the house, a library and guest room, a lavatory, a powder room, and the kitchen. Upstairs are three bedrooms, a dressing room, and two bathrooms.

For summer cooling (and a host of permanent or temporary Washingtonians will sing its praises) the roof surface forms a shallow dead-level water basin around the privacy of a solarium, thus achieving a sense of luxury in spite of Spartan compactness.

The rough stone foundation forms a positive introductory note as a front-yard wall. Inasmuch as glass has the sculptural advantage of suggesting volume when in light and a three-dimensional exposition of the interior when in shade, the fireplace wall of the living room and the screen which backs the dining alcove, both visible from the south, are further recognized and enhanced with glass ornamentation.

The east and west walls, with conventional windows for the sake of privacy, were developed from a design point of view as cheek walls, framing front and rear into rigid panels.

As a practical matter for Washingtonians, who are always having guests, the visitor put up in the curtained-off library alcove will readily recognize the suggested limit of his stay.

ROOF-PLAN

Louis W. Ballou.

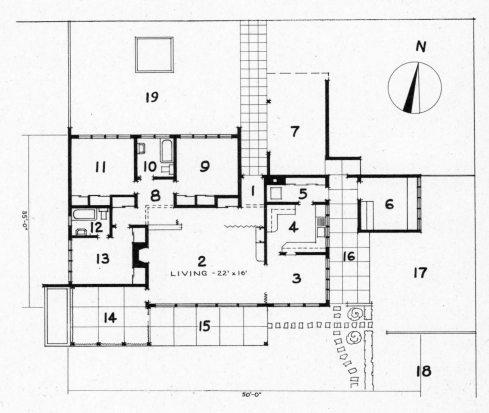

Louis W. Ballou.

VIRGINIA

A. LAWRENCE KOCHER
Architect

A VIRGINIA HOUSE of today differs from a characteristic New England house only in a few special provisions for shade and coolness, requisite in the South, and possibly more accommodations for outdoor living. Otherwise the house of America is the same, whether it be north, south, east, or west.

"Typical Americans," now better acquainted with their compatriots in distant states through improved means of communication, want pretty much the same thing. Their desires are geared by what others have found to be best through reading and experience.

Their proneness to seek the improved is basically the reason for the wide appeal of the solar house. It is more comfortable, more economical to heat, brighter, less confining in aspect; it is simply a better house in which to live.

The Virginia house illustrated herewith has been planned for the comfort and convenience of a typical American family consisting of parents and two children.

The living room is the center and principal room of the house. Its height of twelve feet is in accord with its importance. It provides an area for entertainment, with a plain fireplace surrounded by uncluttered and simple wall space. Opposite is the space for books, for house-

hold records, for reading and writing, available for use as a "collector's corner."

The dining space is part of the living room, readily delineated by a light translucent fabric. It overlooks the rear garden or terrace. The terrace, as directly accessible to the kitchen as is the dining room, also may serve as a dining space. It is toward the east, best suited for the morning meal in the mild morning sun.

A screened porch, a necessity in this climate, is at the southeast corner of the house, to take advantage of the prevailing breeze. It adjoins a covered terrace with adjustable shutters in the roof to admit the winter sun to the living and dining rooms.

This house will be of painted Virginia brick. The large window areas in the living and dining rooms will be of fixed glass, with ventilating louvers below. A ventilating fan pulls air through these louvers and other windows, creating a circulation of air in the desired rooms.

The house will suit its Virginia setting, since it represents the latest solution arrived at by architect and manufacturer to provide for abundant lighting, adequate ventilation, solar heating to supplement the artificial plant in winter, and, at all times, an attractive outlook.

Louis W. Ballou.

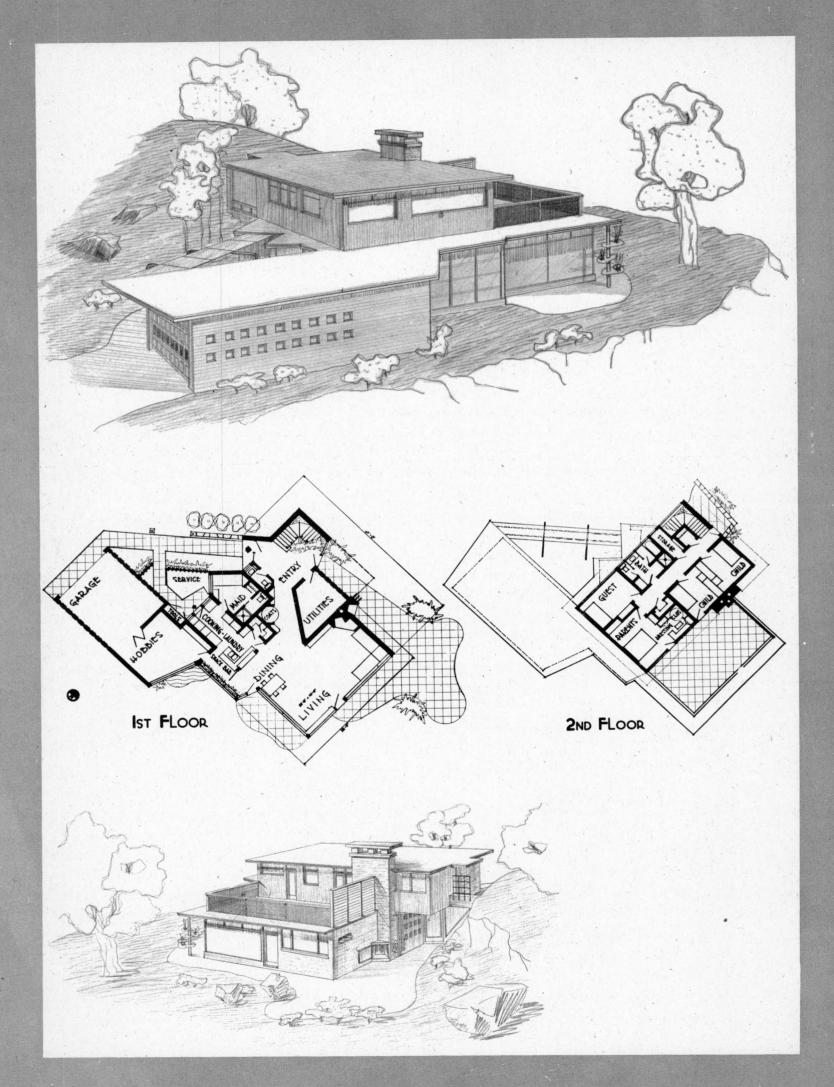

1ST FLOOR

GARAGE

SERVICE

HOBBIES

COOKING-LAUNDRY

MAID

ENTRY

UTILITIES

SNACK BAR

DINING

LIVING

2ND FLOOR

GUEST

PARENTS

BATH

STORAGE

CHILD

CHILD

WEST VIRGINIA

WALTER F. MARTENS
Architect

"THE LITTLE MOUNTAIN STATE" takes its sobriquet from its low mountains and rolling hills, a terrain which provides steep hillsides for most of the available building sites near urban communities. Thus the West Virginia solar house is designed for a rugged and irregular hillside location.

The steep lot presents many problems to architects and builders. Solid-rock outcroppings and ledges at shallow depths make excavation a costly undertaking and a basement an outright waste. The scarcity of level surfaces on such a site dictates the use of a second story for the larger home. More than would be the case with a wide, level lot, entrance driveways, entrance and service courts require compactness. The background barrier of a steep hillside, shading the house for hours each day, complicates the problem of orientation for solar heating.

These factors determined the design and plan of this house. A functional design was selected for full economy in the use of modern materials, for readier adaptability to modern construction methods, and for better installation of present-day equipment.

Flexibility in the use of rooms is a keynote of the design. The entrance hall virtually becomes a garden room with hillside planting visible through large glass areas and with the planting actually carried into the room itself. The dining area can be curtained for privacy or left open as part of the living room. The passageway to the hobby room serves also as a breakfast nook or snack bar, with ready service from the kitchen.

The guest room on the second floor may readily be used as a children's room, while the two rooms specifically allotted to children may be converted into one

large room by changing the portable closet walls to other wall locations. The bathroom may be used by four persons at the same time, thanks to its division into separate areas by partitions and curtains. This arrangement saves the need of a second bathroom upstairs.

In the use of Thermopane for exterior glazing throughout the house except where glass-block panels are shown, its specification has been dictated by other considerations than just the saving of storm sash.

A permanent seal of windows is particularly desirable near the larger industrial centers, to prevent dust infiltration. Air conditioning makes this possible, and use of Thermopane makes the air-conditioning installations more economical. For washing the permanently sealed windows, all exterior surfaces may be reached either from the ground or from roof and deck areas.

In connection with the entrance coatroom and the dressing room off the master bedroom, an ingenious use is made of the commercial type of revolving clothes-hanger rack, to be built into the cabinets.

NORTH CAROLINA

JOHN J. ROWLAND
Architect

THIS HOUSE is designed to gain acceptance as "modern" by the average homeowner and by the average real-estate operator who places style restrictions on the subdivision in which it will be built. It is hoped that the house will advance the course of modern architecture, with all its possibilities and amenities, in this region by *not* going "all the way."

Though the flat or shed roof could have been used here, the sloping roof was adopted with the north eave lower than the eave on the south. This permits natural and forced ventilation over all rooms. A truss spans from exterior wall to exterior wall; ceilings of all rooms slope from the north wall up to the south wall, thus affording better lighted rooms than the usual "A" roof permits.

The plan of the house is simple. All rooms have southern exposure and all but two, the girl's room and the boy's room, have cross-ventilation, and these may be equipped with breeze windows or an exhaust fan may be installed to cool the entire attic, with particular attention to these rooms.

The shelter shown apart from the house is a feature which may be used to advantage in this climate. Screening in summer and Thermopane in winter make it available for year-round use. Here one may play table tennis or other active games. Noisy living is isolated from the house and bedrooms. The problem of cleaning up after parties is simplified. This is an area which, when not used for entertaining, offers quiet solitude and relaxation in an open atmosphere.

Just outside the kitchen, the children have an outdoor play space which in later years may be paved or used for small court games.

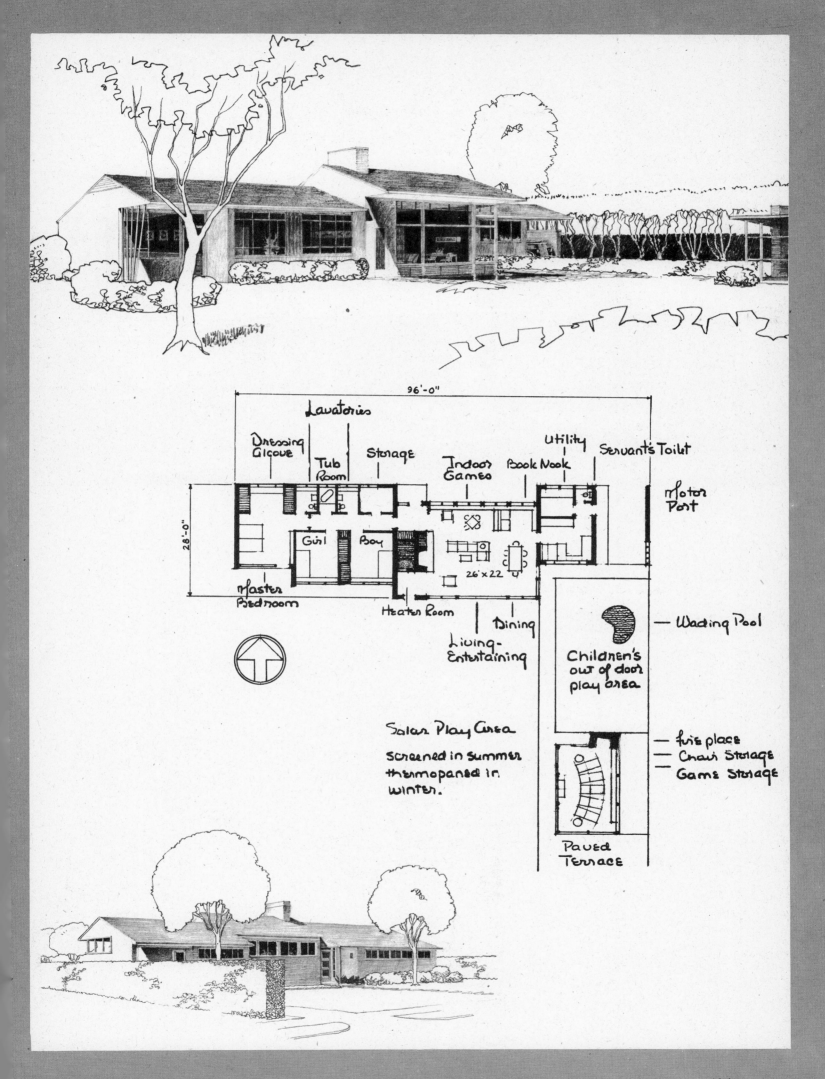

Lavatories

Dressing Alcove

Tub Room

Storage

Indoor Games

Utility

Book Nook

Servant's Toilet

Motor Port

96'-0"

28'-0"

Girl

Boy

26' x 22

Master Bedroom

Heater Room

Living- Entertaining

Dining

Wading Pool

Children's out of door play area

Fire place
Chair Storage
Game Storage

Solar Play Area

Screened in summer thermopaned in winter.

Paved Terrace

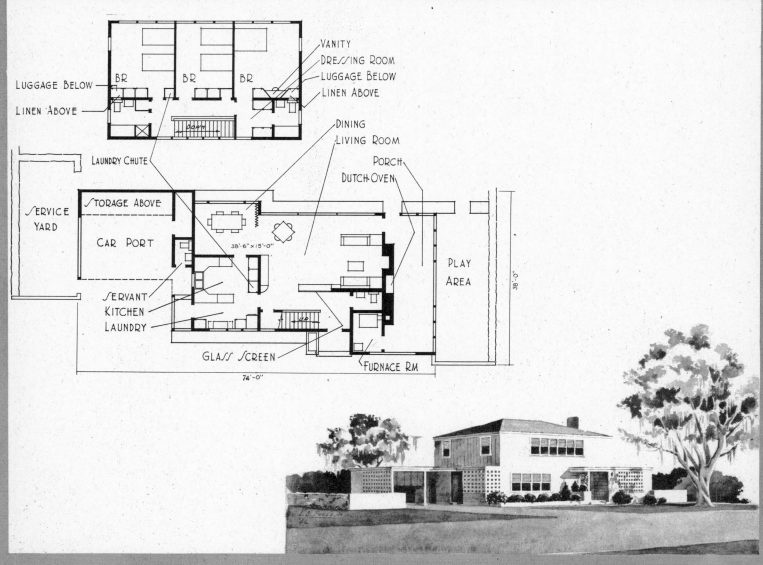

VANITY
DRESSING ROOM
LUGGAGE BELOW
LINEN ABOVE

LUGGAGE BELOW
BR
BR
BR
LINEN ABOVE

LAUNDRY CHUTE

DINING
LIVING ROOM

PORCH
DUTCH OVEN

SERVICE YARD

STORAGE ABOVE

CAR PORT

38'-6"x15'-0"

PLAY AREA

38'-0"

SERVANT
KITCHEN
LAUNDRY

GLASS SCREEN

FURNACE RM

74'-0"

SOUTH CAROLINA

G. THOMAS HARMON 3RD
Architect

THIS STATE tends toward conventional architecture, rejects extreme modern. The designer's objective in this case is the creation of a house generally conventional in character, but with a modern atmosphere.

The house is of wood frame, with gypsum sheathing. The exterior covering is of clapboard applied horizontally on the first floor and vertically on the second. All interior walls and ceilings are of plaster. The flower boxes and garden walls are brick. Space has been left for the addition of an air-conditioning unit which may be connected directly into the air ducts used for heating.

The kitchen and laundry are placed together, separated only by cabinets and range. They are readily accessible to service entrance, drying yard, dining room, front entrance, and stairway to the second floor, making for maximum household operating efficiency with minimum of effort. Storage space has been provided at the rear of the garage, from four feet above the floor, thus utilizing the usual dead space over the hood of the automobile.

The three second-floor bedrooms are large enough for twin beds. The master bedroom has a dressing room adjoining.

The living room is partially separated from the hall by a flower box with translucent glass extending to the ceiling, creating privacy and a sense of spaciousness and decoration.

Living-room and dining-room windows, on the south, are of fixed Thermopane. Ventilation is achieved through slats beneath the living-room windows and on either side of those in the dining room. Second-floor bedroom windows are double-hung. Attic ventilation is gained through the soffit of the second-floor cornice, which also provides exhaust for an attic fan located in the ceiling of the second-floor hall. A laundry chute extends from this hall to the laundry.

The screened porch is partly enclosed with movable shutters, thus affording maximum use in rain or bright sunshine. The play area is adjacent to the porch. A feature of the porch is a Dutch oven. One chimney at this point serves the furnace room, Dutch oven, and living-room fireplace.

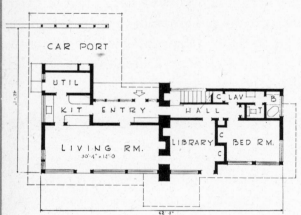

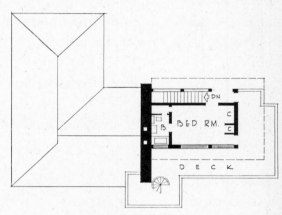

F I R S T   F L O O R

CAR PORT

UTIL

KIT   ENTRY   HALL   C LAV   B

LIVING RM.
30'-4" x 14'-0   LIBRARY   C   BED RM.
C

S E C O N D   F L O O R

DN
BED RM.   C
B   C

D E C K

60

GEORGIA

PRESTON S. STEVENS
Architect

THE SOLAR HOUSE for Georgia was designed in an effort to substitute for the senseless continuation of inappropriate traditional styles a more gracious and pleasant mode of existence in which maximum advantage may be taken of sunlight, openness, view, and a closer relation of indoor and outdoor living.

By proper orientation the sun and breeze are fully utilized. Privacy is achieved by using the service areas of the house to insulate the living areas from the noises and disturbances of the public thoroughfare.

The house opens completely on the south garden, with large expanses of glass in both fixed and movable

Toward this end the traditional small-paned windows were replaced with great expanses of plate glass. Native materials were used to give pleasant warmth of color and texture and a feeling of unity to both interior and exterior treatments.

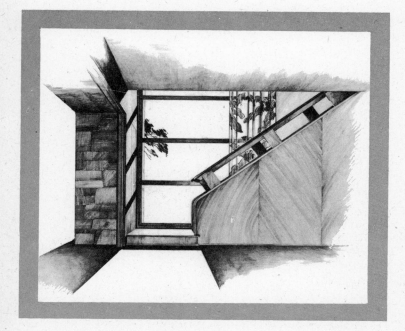

panels which admit light and summer breeze and the attractive garden view.

No separate dining area is provided, since the living room is sufficiently spacious to include it. A counter-height opening between the kitchen and dining space may be used as a snack bar or for meals when more elaborate table setting and serving are not desired. In pleasant weather the terrace affords an additional dining area.

The library adjoining the living area may be used in connection with the living space for entertaining, as a room for guests, or as a quiet retreat for some members of the family when others are entertaining.

The division of toilet facilities on the first floor enables two or three persons to use the space with complete privacy. This is especially desirable when the library is used as a guest room.

The upstairs bedroom may be used as the owner's suite or as a studio. The open deck gives pleasant outdoor space, adequately protected by the overhanging roof.

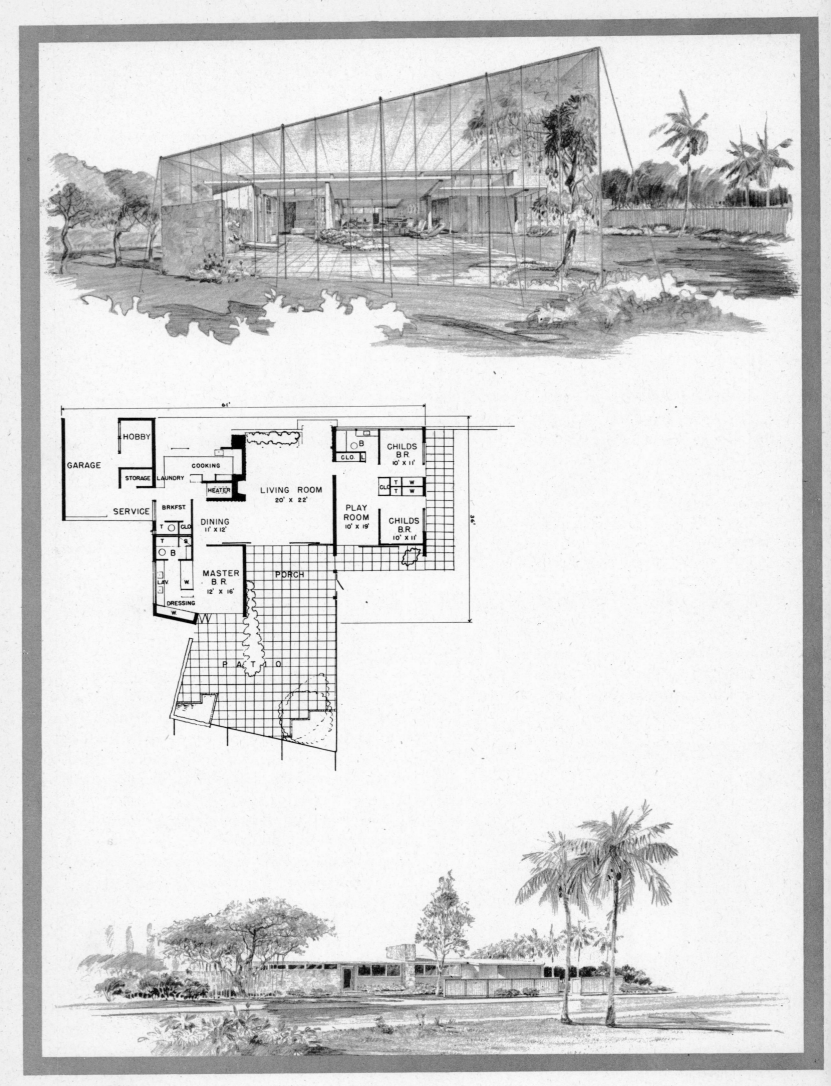

HOBBY

GARAGE

STORAGE LAUNDRY COOKING

HEATER

SERVICE

BRKFST.

DINING
11' x 12'

LIVING ROOM
20' x 22'

PLAY
ROOM
10' x 19'

CHILDS
B.R.
10' x 11'

CLO. B

CLO

CHILDS
B.R.
10' x 11'

MASTER
B.R.
12' x 16'

PORCH

DRESSING

PATIO

FLORIDA

ROBERT LAW WEED
Architect

THE SOUTHEAST TRADE WINDS offer a pleasant temperature the year around in semitropical Florida if the architect takes full and careful advantage of cross-ventilation and makes provision to admit solar heat for December and January.

Thus windows to the south, and particularly the clerestory windows, admit sun to the living room, dining room, and playroom for an hour or so at the middle of the day in December, January, and early February. During the winter months from November to March, the very early-morning sun is admitted to the dining room.

With a warm winter sun, infrequent frosts, and never any snow, Florida offers a chance for the fullest of living out-of-doors. Insects also find such a prospect attractive at night, but they are easily circumvented by provision of a screened patio or terrace.

Construction is simply a series of twenty-foot spans, spanning east and west. This permits large south and north openings so necessary to cross-ventilation. The south walls are sliding glass doors to permit maximum openings. The north walls are opened by sliding windows, forty inches or more from the floor, which extend the full width of the twenty-foot bay. Thus the fullest ventilation and also privacy from the streets are provided.

The house has been designed on the zoning principle. The children have their sleeping rooms and playroom adjacent to a play yard. This yard may be completely separated from the other activities of the house or used as an auxiliary entertaining area in conjunction with living room and patio. The living room, dining room, porch, and patio combine as one large party area and make entertaining on a grand scale possible. The master suite is placed to enable mother and father to retire to their quarters for undisturbed comfort.

The work zone is designed for cooking, laundry, and light meals. Adjacent to it are large general storage facilities, a hobby room, and a service yard. A carport type of garage, without doors, and screened from the street by fence and gates, shelters the family car.

Attention is called to the large coils under glass which collect the sun's rays and help to heat the domestic water supply.

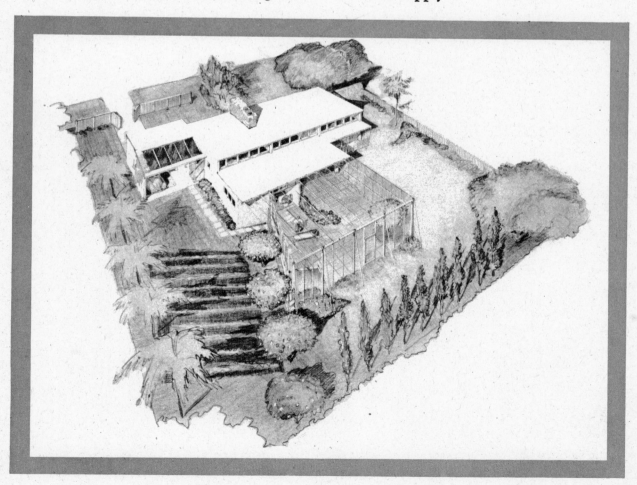

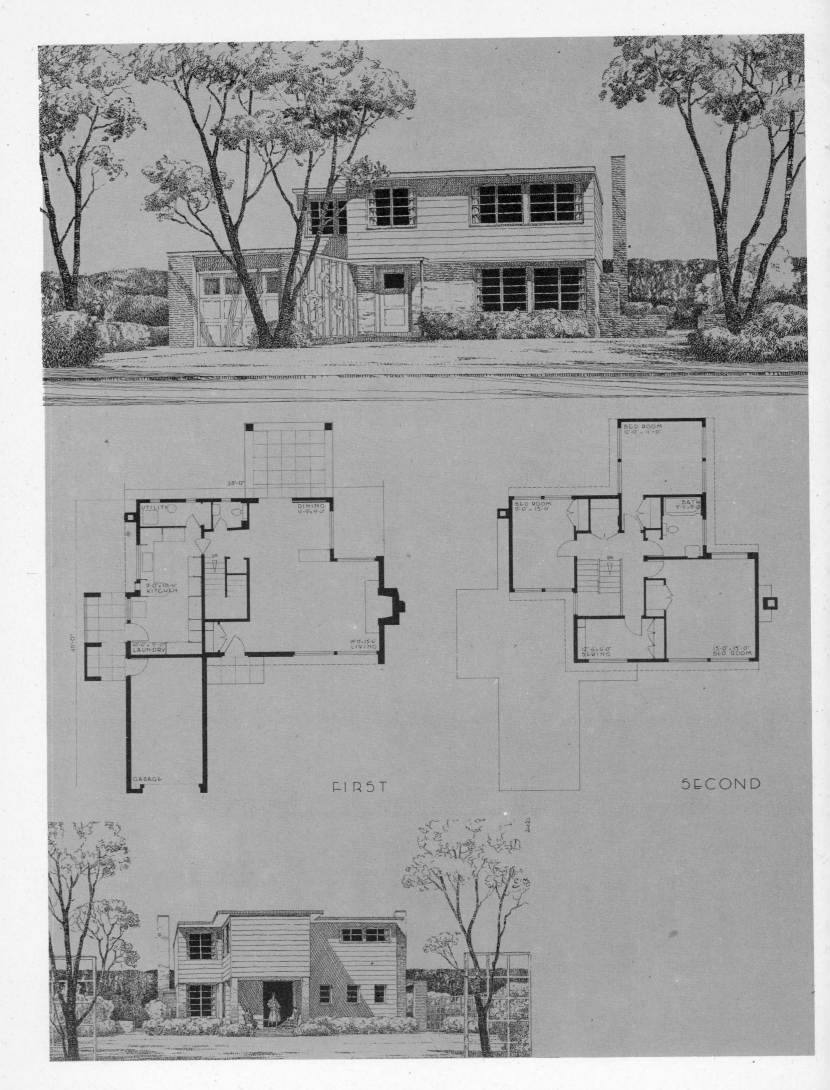

FIRST

SECOND

OHIO

J. BYERS HAYS
Architect

VIEWPOINTS on housing today range from those based primarily on sentimental and traditional architectural fantasies at the expense of realism to those intent on devising a "machine for living" which concentrates on engineering perfection in an endeavor to produce an acceptable human domestic environment.

The social, economic, and aesthetic standards and demands which comprise the human activity of families are too diverse to permit a simple formula. This solution, therefore, is suggested only as one man's viewpoint, presented in the hope that it may contribute in some measure to solving the problems of others.

Most families live in urban or suburban communities. In general their houses will stand on lots approximately 5000 to 7000 square feet. The layout of streets in allotted areas has been more concerned with the quantity of subdivided lots than with orientation, view, and other factors which contribute to desirable home-building sites. The designers of the Ohio solar house accept these realistic conditions rather than select arbitrarily an ideal countryside site.

Thus the following conditions were adopted:

Use of the lot and placement of the building on it so that a maximum of sunshine, air, and general openness, as well as a degree of privacy for the occupants, is provided—all of these are too frequently ignored in the majority of homes.

A disposition of internal space arrangement which logically provides for the various activities of family life, recreation, eating, sleeping, and a work center for household duties, in their most convenient relation, one to another.

Constant consideration not only of the initial economies of investment but also of the items of upkeep cost and physical labor required to operate and maintain a home.

Combining the living and dining areas makes possible a maximum space for entertainment yet permits partial division of the area through the use of a screen or curtain so that privacy for specific activities is possible. The work center, combining kitchen and laundry areas, permits efficient household operation; the center is conveniently located to permit easy service to dining area or porch and attention to the many other activities

of housekeeping. The porch offers the maximum of exposure required of outdoor living room.

The second floor provides well-cross-ventilated sleeping rooms for a family of four. A guest room, used only occasionally, was eliminated in the interest of economy. A temporary doubling up or a cot in the sewing room could accommodate the occasional overnight visitor.

The external expression of the house relies on a pleasing disposition of mass and fenestration dictated by the interior arrangement rather than by a predetermined idea based on the application of superfluous architecture.

CAR BERTH
AND WORKSHOP

KITCHEN

B.R. BATH

22'×15'
LIVING
ROOM

B.R. B.R.

PORCH

DINETTE

70'-6"

MICHIGAN

ALDEN B. DOW
Architect

FORM always develops from the materials and purpose of the structure.

The fundamental purpose of a house is to provide space for the development of family life.

Such a space must, first of all, offer protection from heat and cold and provide an efficient handling of the physical routine of living. In addition it must offer privacy and a freedom in which the occupant may develop as an individual.

The job of the architect is to provide this space and to arrange it in a manner to inspire the natural and healthy growth of the individuals living in it.

The Michigan solar house is a happy house because it is natural. It is an exciting one because it is colorful, spacious, and alive with the movement of nature.

In Michigan the winters are cold and the summers are hot. Each season has its own peculiar beauty of form and color. In this house the large windows and entire walls of glass bring that beauty inside. The plan and roof are arranged to flood every room except the front bathroom with the low winter sun, while in summer each room will be shielded by the roof overhang and deciduous plantings.

The automobile, as important equipment for present-day life, gets a storage space not only handy for operation but accessible to the various parts of the house. This space is called the car *berth* because it is used only for storing the car at *night*. At other times it is used for playroom, workshop, or laundry. It has direct access to the kitchen and hall connecting the bedrooms, living room, and front door.

The front door is well protected by an overhanging roof which provides a covered entrance for automobile passengers. The hall onto which it opens, together with the passage to the screen porch, defines clearly the path of circulation through the house, thereby giving maximum freedom to the lounging, living, and quiet centers. The living room is separated from the porch by high double-hung sash which, when opened, provides a clear area through the house to the porch. This gives a very large living space during the hot summer months when spaciousness is most desirable.

The part of the porch under the high ceiling provides an excellent space for hanging plants which, in the wintertime, may be fixed from the high ceiling inside and flooded with winter sun. The early-morning summer sun is brought into this living space through roof windows on the north side.

Planting or landscaping is an essential part of the house. Not only does it create a pleasant shade for the windows in summer, but, most important, it provides a constant, living change that animates the house to something beyond mere physical functional space.

You will find this house livable and workable, providing also that essential *plus* for better living—the kind of space that is inspiring to human growth.

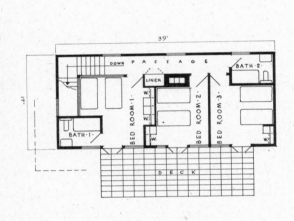

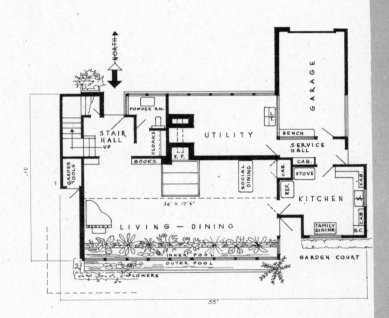

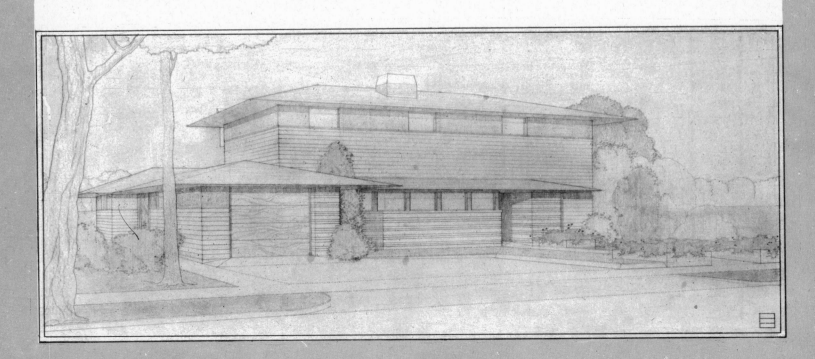

68

INDIANA

JOHN LLOYD WRIGHT
Architect

THE NATURAL SCENERY of Indiana has inspired so many poets, so many writers of songs, that I have never been able to understand why the Indiana homeowner does not demand that same inspiration for the house he builds. Much of the state is truly beautiful, whether it be the dunes of the north, the many small, clear lakes of the pastoral northeast, the tumbling hills and narrow woodland valleys of Brown County, or the land along the Ohio River toward the south; I have tried to make that scenic beauty as much a part of this house as the limestone so plentiful in Indiana.

This house is designed for a family of four—father, mother, and two children. It is to stand on a lot of at least seventy-five feet. All "living" areas—living-dining room, bedroom, kitchen—are exposed to the south. A stationary glass area runs the full length of the living-dining room's south wall, along both inside and outside of which is a pool extending the full length of the room. It provides a handsome background for exciting plant and flower arrangements, lends color, and yields a desirable humidity.

The wall finish of this room provides what rightfully may be termed an "enclosed exterior." It is of cedar shingles and stratified limestone. At the north end of the room are stonewalled fireplace, warm stone hearth, and built-in bookcases.

The north side of the house shields the occupants from the street. East and west walls, opposite the adjoining property lines, are closed for privacy and for protection from the rays of the eastern and western sun, which cannot be controlled by solar mechanics as can the sun's rays from the south.

Special solar canopies are designed to permit the sun's rays to penetrate one hundred per cent of the glass areas during the coldest season and to shut them out completely during the hottest.

In addition, I have provided special solar "drops," which consist of pipe frames covered with canvas. These are hinged to the netherside of the stationary canopies and controlled by cords. They may be pulled up flush to the surface of the stationary canopy or lowered arcwise to any desired angle. These "drops" permit shelter from the sun's rays at any time, and provide a practical and attractive solution to the problem of total solar control.

Glass areas throughout the house are of fixed Thermopane, to provide maximum economy of construction and upkeep, insulation and solar benefits, to create a draftless, dustless house, and to eliminate the use of window screens.

Ventilation is provided by door openings and the mechanical circulation of air.

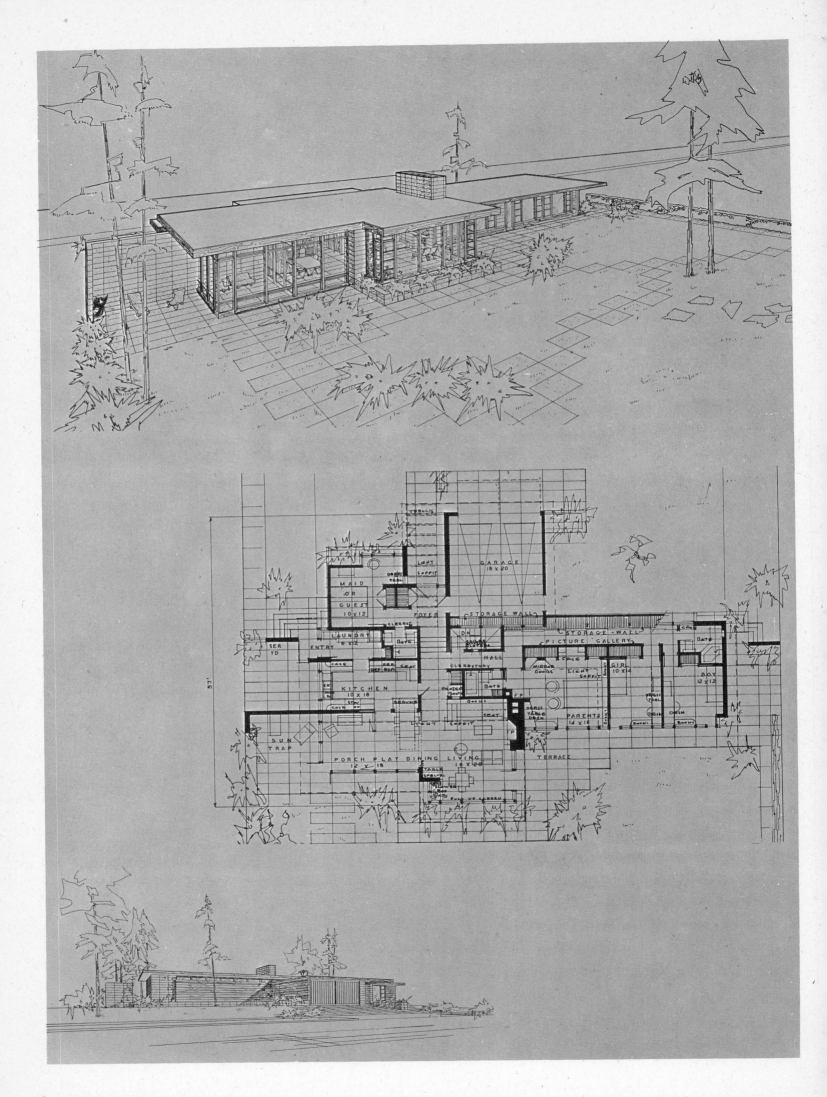

WISCONSIN

WILLIAM V. KAESER
Architect

THE MODERN ORGANIC HOUSE must concern itself with a complex set of conditions. It must meet the needs of family life of today. It must provide protection from the elements. It must fit into its surroundings. It must meet the requirements of a set of structural, hygienic, and safety standards. It must provide the maximum of ease in operation and upkeep, and it *should* give its occupants the chance to enjoy their natural surroundings to the utmost without loss of privacy or comfort.

Thus, it can be understood that a modern house should be a flexible, easily adjusted organism, since it concerns itself directly with the life within.

In a family of four or five there generally will be a variety of interests and friends. In this connection a philosophical observation is pertinent: "The reality of a house is not its solid sticks and stones, but the space within."

In the design of a small house, it is necessary to make the space serve a variety of activities.

A feature of this house is the development of the master bedroom as a subsidiary living room. Fitted with its own fireplace, work desk, and plenty of space for several easy chairs, it provides an inviting and comfortable retreat for the parents when the children grow up and use the main living portion to entertain.

The weather in Wisconsin is always variable; it ranges from extreme cold to extreme heat. The true house of Wisconsin should be built to meet these condi-tions. In this house there is a variety of ventilators. It can be practically sealed shut in winter or completely opened in the summer, through the use of awning or louver-type sash and fixed panels of Thermopane and suitable heating—practically any combination of conditions can be met. A sudden rain will always find everything protected. The house is almost entirely closed on the north, against the prevailing winter winds, and entirely glazed on the south, to take advantage of solar heating in the winter and the prevailing winds in the summer. Through the use of Thermopane, the heat loss on dark days would not be excessive. The long, flat shape makes the whole house virtually a sun trap.

I have endeavored to make this house the direct expression of its structure as well as its function. In other words, I have tried to bring form and function into one. The materials and their manner of use produce the design, decoration, and color scheme. There is nothing here that is added on. The materials here are chosen for their decorative as well as their structural qualities. This house is designed largely of stock materials and based on a module system, so that it can be partially prefabricated or largely precut.

The house flows freely and easily to the out-of-doors and, through the extension of the concrete mat into the terraces, becomes unified with the garden. It can be sealed up completely, without affecting the visual enjoyment of the natural surroundings.

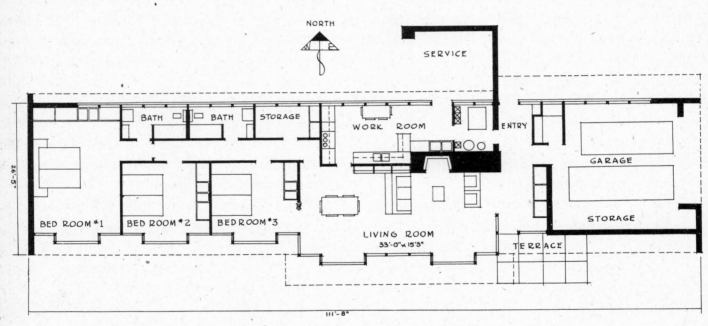

NORTH

SERVICE

BATH BATH STORAGE

WORK ROOM

ENTRY

GARAGE

BED ROOM #1 BED ROOM #2 BEDROOM #3

LIVING ROOM
33'-0" x 15'3"

STORAGE

TERRACE

26'-5"

111'-8"

ILLINOIS

GEORGE FRED KECK
Architect

THE MEANING of the solar house, analytically, is the fact of designing a house to fit the climate into which it is to be placed. By climate I mean all the weather conditions encountered in the specific region.

For the Illinois solar house, the first and most important of the weather conditions is the act of the sun. The house is designed to exclude and prevent the sun from entering through the glass in the summer, when there is too much solar radiation. It is designed to admit the sun in winter. To this end, all the important rooms for living are placed to face the south.

The area of glass proportions for each room is nearly a constant, so that in winter the same proportionate amount of sun will strike each room, warming it uniformly and proportionately with the others during the time the sun is up. Only the secondary rooms, in which artificial heat is desired, face north.

In winter the colder winds come from the northwest, north, and northeast. The secondary rooms on the north act as buffers against these frigid blasts. In summer the prevailing winds of Illinois are from the southwest, and they are able then to help the living quarters with their welcome breezes. In other words, this house sensibly turns its back on the cold winter winds and opens its jacket to cooling breezes in summertime.

There is a through entry hall next to the garage, just as in the early houses of tidewater Virginia. It gives equal emphasis to the front or street entry and the garden entry.

The living and dining rooms are combined into one large room. Sleeping quarters consist of a large master bedroom and two smaller bedrooms.

Behind the louvered ventilators are copper screens which remain in place the year around. The louvers keep the rain out and make it unnecessary to close the house tight when the family goes away for a few days. Many such ventilators are opened in the spring and not closed until the fall.

The exterior of the house is of brick and wood. Stone may be substituted as desired.

The living-room ceiling has been raised for added height in this large room and to provide clerestory lighting and ventilation all around the room.

The roof is flat and designed to hold a sheet of water which, by its evaporation, helps to keep the interior cool on scorching summer days when the sun glares down on it. An inside downspout runs off excess water, with no outside gutters or downspouts needed.

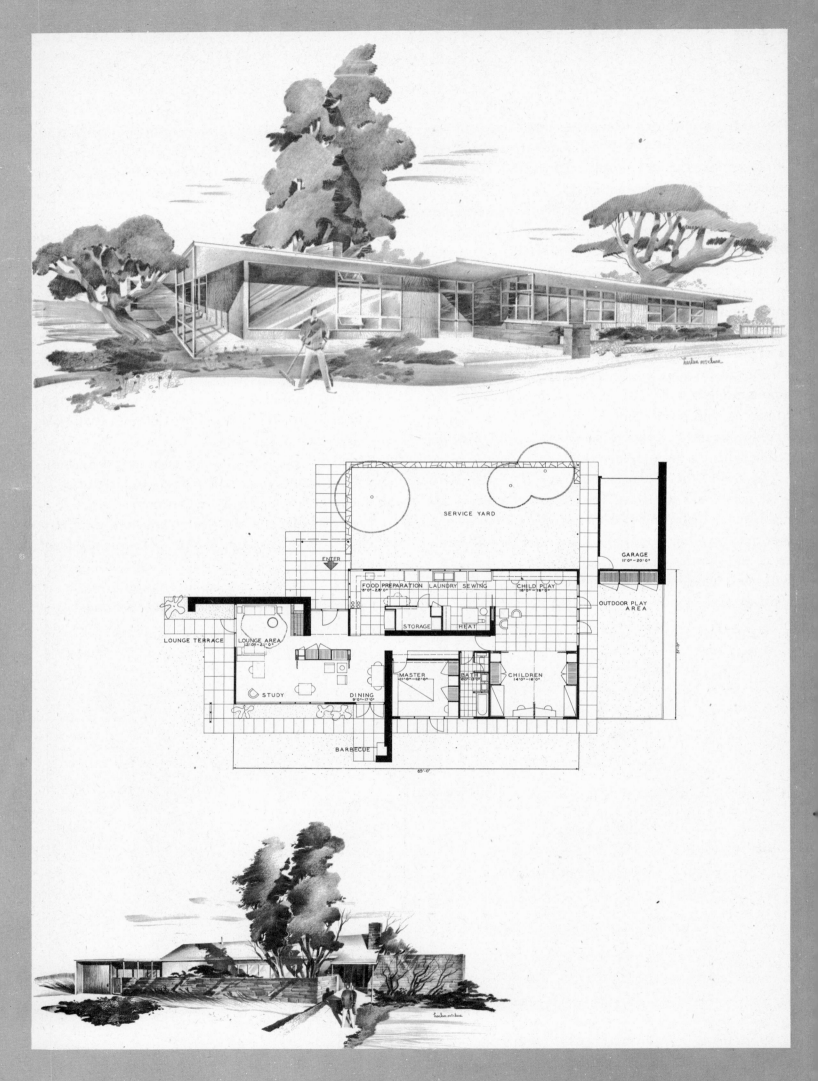

SERVICE YARD

GARAGE
11'0"–20'0"

ENTER

FOOD PREPARATION   LAUNDRY SEWING   CHILD PLAY
8'0"–28'0"   14'0"–18'0"

OUTDOOR PLAY
AREA

STORAGE   HEAT

LOUNGE TERRACE   LOUNGE AREA
                 12'0"–21'0"

STUDY

                  DINING   MASTER   BATH   CHILDREN
                  9'0"–17'0"   14'0"–12'0"   6'0"–9'0" 14'0"–18'0"

BARBECUE

65'-0"

MINNESOTA

ROBERT G. CERNY
Architect

THE SOLAR HOUSE for independent, hearty, wide-shouldered Minnesota was planned with the thought in mind that in the future most households will not have domestic help.

This means that the housewife will have a full-time job as operating engineer of the home and supervisor of her children's play. The happiness and peace of mind of all concerned will be enhanced if the youngsters can be kept within their mother's line of vision but out from under her feet.

In consequence of this, directly outside the children's sleeping quarters and adjacent to the kitchen is a large, free, gay, and open play area. A gate divides it from the kitchen.

On one side of the closed gate the housewife may

the area as a study or a hobby space, and later convert it into a more grown-up rumpus room.

At the north end of the L-shaped living room, the least bright part of the room, we have put the fireplace, deep back and sheltered, to provide a cozy area about it that offers a happy refuge on some of our Minnesota winter nights.

The dining room off the opposite side of the living room is arranged to serve the usual family group comfortably, but the table may be extended quite deep into the living room without sacrificing the privacy of the dining area.

The master bedroom is an isolated unit. At the end of the house devoted to the children we show two rooms and the play area. It is our idea that this space may

carry on all her domestic chores while giving the youngsters, on the other side, the companionship, security, and guidance that her presence affords.

On their side, the children may leave their toys about and romp wholeheartedly without disturbing the operation of the household. We have often been ruefully reminded that there is no point whatever in building an efficient kitchen if its floor is to be littered constantly with blocks, toys, and other hazards.

The playroom, moreover, is a through-the-years proposition. As the children become older they may use

be divided in any desired manner. A house frequently being a lifetime adventure, many parents have found their home too large for comfort or economy when their children have departed for homes of their own. The flexibility of the children's wing here makes possible its later adaptation to several uses, even subdivision into a small apartment for other tenants.

All the principal living areas face the south. The kitchen, laundry, and play area are behind them, but the roof is developed to admit the south light to these rooms on a clerestory level.

IOWA

AMOS B. EMERY
Architect

Iowa is a level land of fertile farms, geometrically patterned fields of corn and wheat, towering silos, white houses, big red barns, town skylines broken by church steeples and grain elevators, great stretches wrapped in the yellow light of prairie. Although many of them leave it for other abodes, Iowans love the land, and hominess is the greatest common denominator of their tastes and requirements in a house.

This house was designed for a family of four—father, mother, son and daughter—and was planned basically for a lot with a fine view to the south and the public street to the north, although, keeping its open side to the sun, it might be placed on a lot facing any direction.

In my experience I have found that most people like a living room which is just that, not an entrance or a passage, but an area in which to assemble family and friends in a group uninterrupted by other travel into or about the house. Thus, the living room in the Iowa house is up three steps, the better to separate it from the other part of the house.

I have also found that many American women, with the help of modern equipment, choose to do their own laundry, and so a laundry room has been included. For maximum convenience it is next to the kitchen, on the ground floor.

The playroom is not an absolute necessity, but it is a good long-term investment in family comfort and building conservation. When the children are young it gives them a ready play space when bad weather drives them indoors. When they are in their teens, it becomes a recreation room in which they and their chums can dance without tearing up the living room. It also saves their parents from the rather limited choice of participation in young people's frolic or forced retreat to the bedroom.

The children's bedrooms, on the south, are arranged for use as study rooms, and have double-deck beds, in lieu of a guest room, to accommodate overnight visitors.

The panel between the hall and dining room, and in the stair rail, affords light and sparkle to the hallway. The glass doors and shelves in the upper part of the built-in dish-and-linen cupboard provide an excellent opportunity to use the better china pieces for their decorative value. A large mirror over the mantel adds a look of greater spaciousness to the living room and reflects a picture of the outdoors.

Should a cut in the over-all price of the house be necessary, the heater room could occupy the storage space at the end of the garage and the basement could be eliminated.

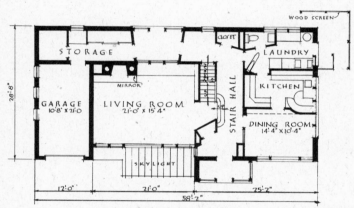

STORAGE

GARAGE
10'-8" x 21'-0"

LIVING ROOM
21'-0" x 15'-4"

MIRROR

CLOSET

LAUNDRY

WOOD SCREEN

KITCHEN

STAIR HALL

DINING ROOM
14'-4" x 10'-4"

SKYLIGHT

26'-8"

12'-0"   21'-0"   25'-2"
58'-2"

FIRST FLOOR PLAN

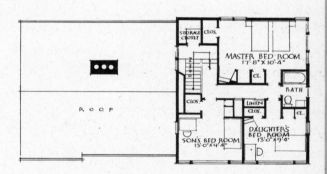

ROOF

STORAGE CLOSET

MASTER BED ROOM
17'-8" x 10'-4"

CL.

CLOS.

BATH

LINEN CLOS.

CL.

SON'S BED ROOM
13'-0" x 4'-4"

DAUGHTER'S BED ROOM
13'-0" x 9'-4"

SECOND FLOOR PLAN

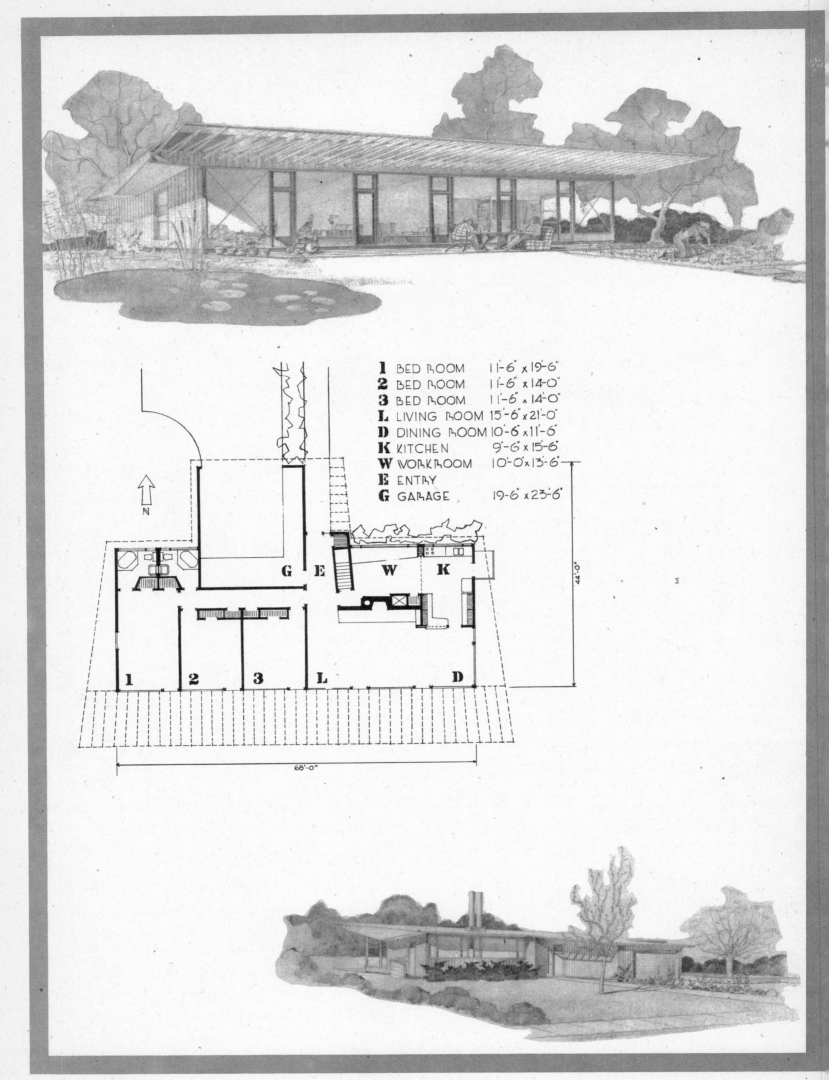

1 BED ROOM 11'-6" x 19'-6"
2 BED ROOM 11'-6" x 14'-0"
3 BED ROOM 11'-6" x 14'-0"
L LIVING ROOM 15'-6" x 21'-0"
D DINING ROOM 10'-6" x 11'-6"
K KITCHEN 9'-6" x 15'-6"
W WORKROOM 10'-0" x 13'-6"
E ENTRY
G GARAGE 19'-6" x 23'-6"

MISSOURI

HARRIS ARMSTRONG
Architect

THE MISSOURI ARCHITECT of today is heir to the traditions of many national groups, to the structures of the French, the half-timbered houses of the Germans, the buildings from the classic revival. He works in a varied region of Ozark plateau and cotton plantation, grain-laden prairie and blue-grass pasture, and of such varied

Artificial lighting will be integrated into the design, and the kitchen and adjoining workroom are to be furnished with complete electrical equipment. The workroom may be used for laundry, sewing, preserving, ping-pong, informal snacks, or other features of informal entertaining.

people as mountaineers and miners, business bosses in skyscraper offices, river men in shanty boats.

Against this wide-ranging background, the Missouri architect today works with a growing emphasis on the functional, with a longer thought to the ultimate purpose of the structure which he designs.

This solar house is planned for livability, comfort, and efficiency and, through integration of the interior with the spacious gifts of the out-of-doors, for freedom from any sense of confinement.

In this house there will be several features not readily apparent in the drawings. There is a seasonal lag between the sun and the mean average temperature. In Missouri this amounts to about thirty-four days, and in order to get shade from the eaves until the first of October (which is desirable here) and still enjoy the spring sunshine until about April 1, this design contemplates use of a strip of plastic-coated fabric, laced between eyelets at the outer edge of the roof projection.

The exterior of the house will be finished in natural oiled red cypress. It will be topped with a sea-green slate-coated asphalt cap sheet over a built-up roof.

Since the entire south face of the building is to be of glass, crossed steel cables in the two end glass panels are used to obtain stability. These three-eighths-of-an-inch cables will not mar the sense of openness at these locations.

Plant materials used for landscaping at or near the lot lines should be very dense, and where views of neighboring houses would be undesirable, fast-growing evergreens might well be used. In general, the landscaping will have to be designed around the individual owner's preferences since these vary much more than the functional requirements within the house.

Wherever possible, the construction methods employed are the accepted standards of the industry, since too great a variation from these standards is always reflected in disproportionately higher building costs.

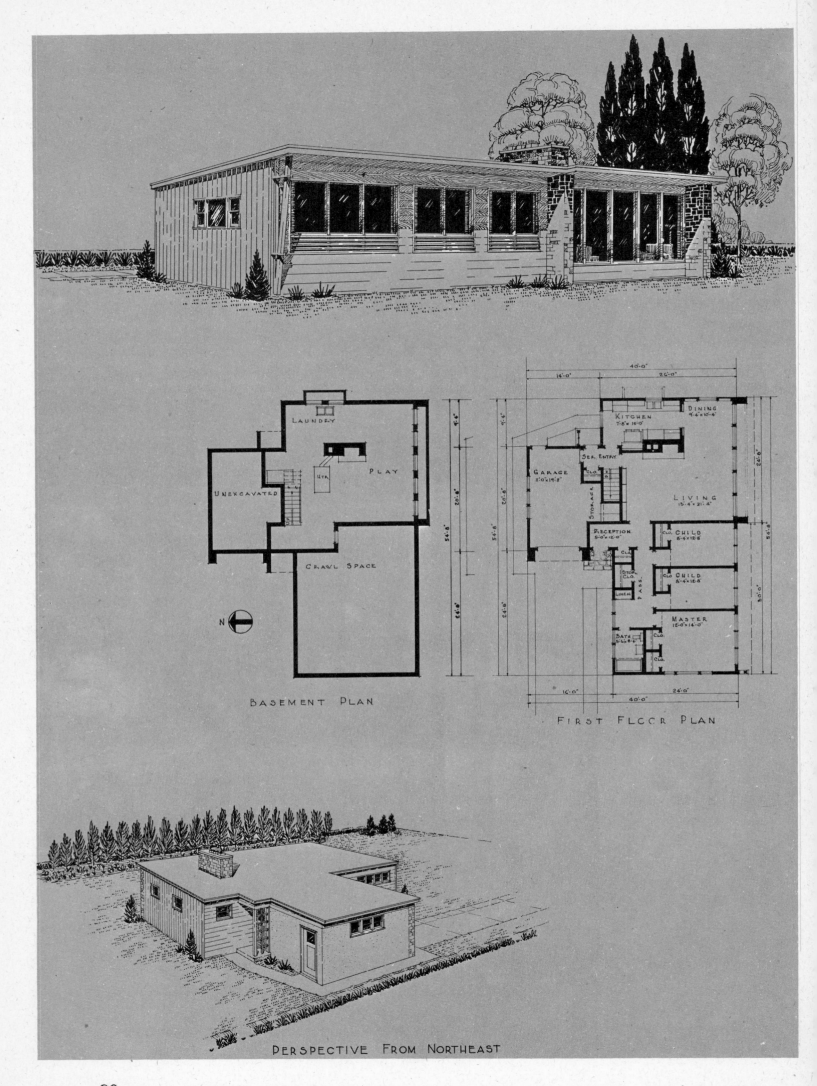

BASEMENT PLAN

FIRST FLOOR PLAN

PERSPECTIVE FROM NORTHEAST

NORTH DAKOTA

HAROLD E. BECHTEL
Architect

THE NORTH DAKOTA solar house lifts its south face to the sun. The south wall, with its large Thermopane areas, is the highest wall of the house, to provide ample glass with the simple framing of ordinary construction practices. All service rooms are on the north as a buffer against prevailing winter winds, and the north wall is the lowest in the house, providing a minimum of wall exposure. It is only logical, therefore, to pitch the roof in one direction, from the high south side to the low north side.

Since most streets in residential districts of North Dakota cities and towns run north and south, this house was designed with a west front for a wide lot. With this arrangement, flower gardens and screen planting would be placed at the south side of the property. Simply by reversing this plan the house may be built on an east front lot.

The bedroom wing is designed as a separate unit, which may be reached directly from the reception hall without passing through any other room. The living room is entered either from the reception hall or from the service entry, which also provides access to the kitchen, basement stairway, and garage.

Because of cost considerations, the laundry, a play area, and the heater room are placed in the basement below the living-room area. A heated crawl space is provided under the bedroom wing to give access to plumbing pipes and heating ducts and to eliminate cold bathroom and bedroom floors.

The living room is extended along the south to provide a dining alcove. The kitchen is connected to the dining alcove by a wide opening equipped with glazed sliding doors.

Upper wall cabinets of the kitchen have sliding glass doors, and lower cabinets are recessed below the top drawers to provide leg room for persons who prefer to work from a stool.

The plan for this house develops a zone-controlled duct system for heating. The rooms on the south, receiving solar heat, constitute two zones—the living room and dining room, one, and the bedrooms the second. All other rooms are included in a third zone. Thermostatically controlled dampers govern the heat as required in various zones, making uniform heating possible throughout the house and functioning in perfect coordination with the heat provided by the sun.

Exterior walls are covered with redwood boards, redwood siding, and stucco with stone trim.

LANDSCAPE PLAN
FROM SOUTHWEST

SOUTH DAKOTA

HAROLD SPITZNAGEL
Architect

TOO OFTEN the average home builder is more concerned with constructing a residence that will inspire the praise of the passer-by than he is with offering his family the best possible arrangement for living. This house was designed primarily for the convenience of its residents, and not necessarily for its appeal to passing motorists.

The service portion of the house, including garage, utility room, kitchen, and drying yard are all toward the front, leaving the rear or garden side of the residence entirely for the owner's enjoyment. The glass is allotted on this same basis, with a minimum on the street side, to afford privacy, and a maximum of glass to open on the controlled view.

The kitchen and utility rooms are located to enable the housewife to reach the entrance or service doors with a minimum of walking, whether she is working in the kitchen or the laundry. The drying yard, while screened from the street and from the garden, is readily accessible to the laundry itself. The porch, screened from the kitchen, offers the opportunity for summertime outdoor dining with minimum effort.

The stone-paved entrance vestibule is especially desirable during bad weather, and the incoming guest is saved from the embarrassment of walking on his heels to protect a fine carpet which often extends right up to the threshold.

The bedroom wing offers cross-ventilation of two of the three rooms and is entirely separate from the remainder of the house. High bathroom windows provide the best light for shaving.

For the exterior, V-groove vertical boards, of uniform or random width, are indicated. Monoslope roofs are specified for all areas except that of the connecting passage formed by the utility room and entranceway.

parents

boy

study

living

dining

girl

bath

kitchen

utility

drying

garage

vegetables

24'

32'

5'6'

27'

12'

17'

12'

12'

20'

20'

0 5' 10' 20'

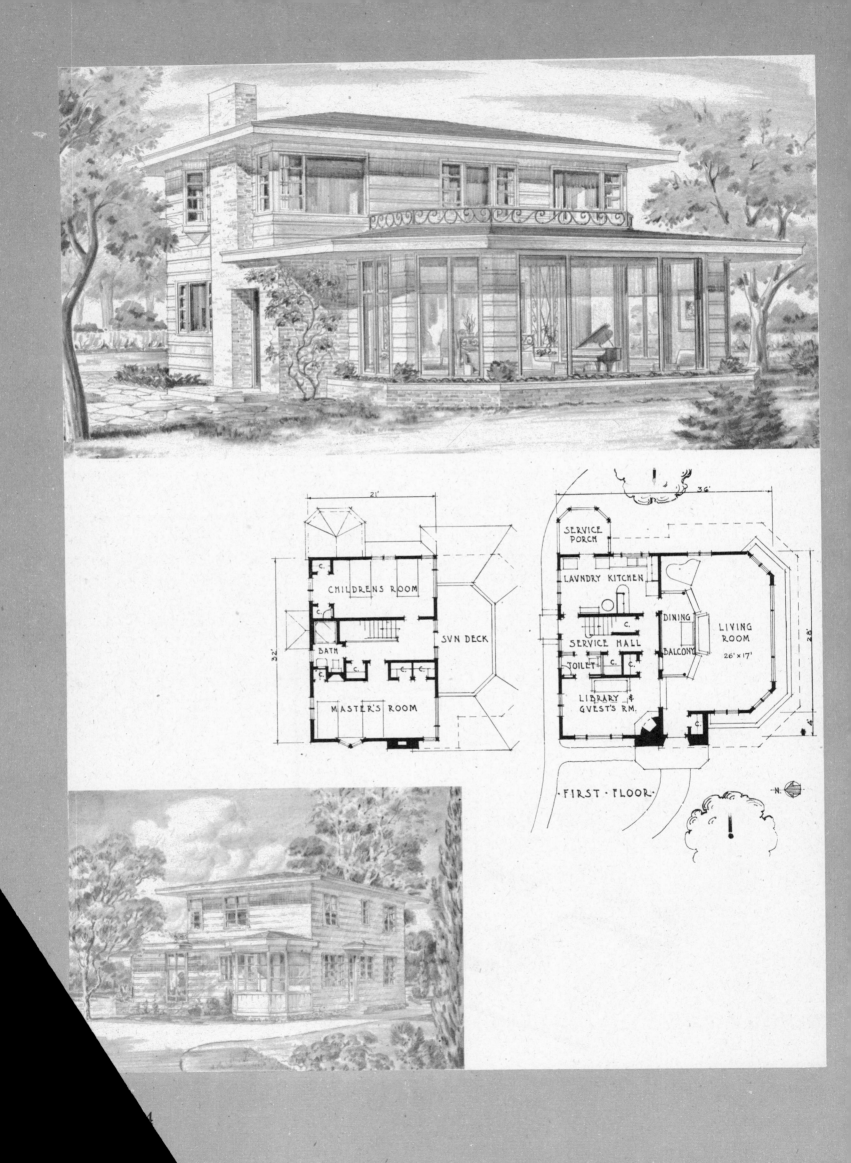

CHILDRENS ROOM

SUN DECK

BATH

MASTER'S ROOM

21'

32'

SERVICE PORCH

LAUNDRY KITCHEN

SERVICE HALL

DINING

BALCONY

TOILET

LIBRARY & GUEST'S RM.

LIVING ROOM 26'x17'

36'

28'

FIRST FLOOR

N

NEBRASKA

NORMAN R. BRIGHAM
Architect

AN ARCHITECT, when planning a house, takes into consideration and specifies, when expedient, the materials native to the locale in which it is to be built. He is also influenced by the climate, the topography of the region, and the orientation of the house on the site. In designing this solar house for Nebraska, I have taken full advantage of the high percentage of days with sunshine which characterize this state. By the extensive use of glass, the great outdoors, with its rolling plains and distant scenery, has been integrated into the structure of this house.

The living room of the Nebraska house has glazed exposures on all three outer walls, with ample ventilation through four pairs of hinged casement windows. These large glass areas provide an expansive view of the surrounding landscape to the south, east, and west.

Incorporated in the living room and benefiting from these views is a dining balcony screened at the sides with iron grillwork and backed by a large mirror reflecting the garden scene.

A library, with a corner fireplace, opens off the living room and may be enclosed from it by sliding decorated glass doors. The library may also serve as a guest room or a dining room.

The kitchen, as well as all the other rooms, has a full quota of sunlight, good ventilation, and garden view. It also contains the laundry facilities, partially concealed by a decorated glass partition, and the water heater. The adjacent, glassed-in service porch may be used as a breakfast room or as a drying room for the laundry.

A service hall with exterior entrance is the main artery of the house, conveniently accessible to all the rooms. It has an adjacent toilet, cloak closet, kitchen entrance, and stairway, all concealed from the living room.

The master bedroom, on the second floor, has exposures on three sides, with a broad view of the garden. It has three closets. The children's room, across the hall, has the same light, airy atmosphere, and benefits as well from the heat of the sun's rays in wintertime. The hall between has a bathroom at the north end, and at the south a glass wall with a glass door opening onto a sun deck above the living room. A convenient lavatory is provided in one of the two closets in the children's room.

This house has been expressly designed for an urban site.

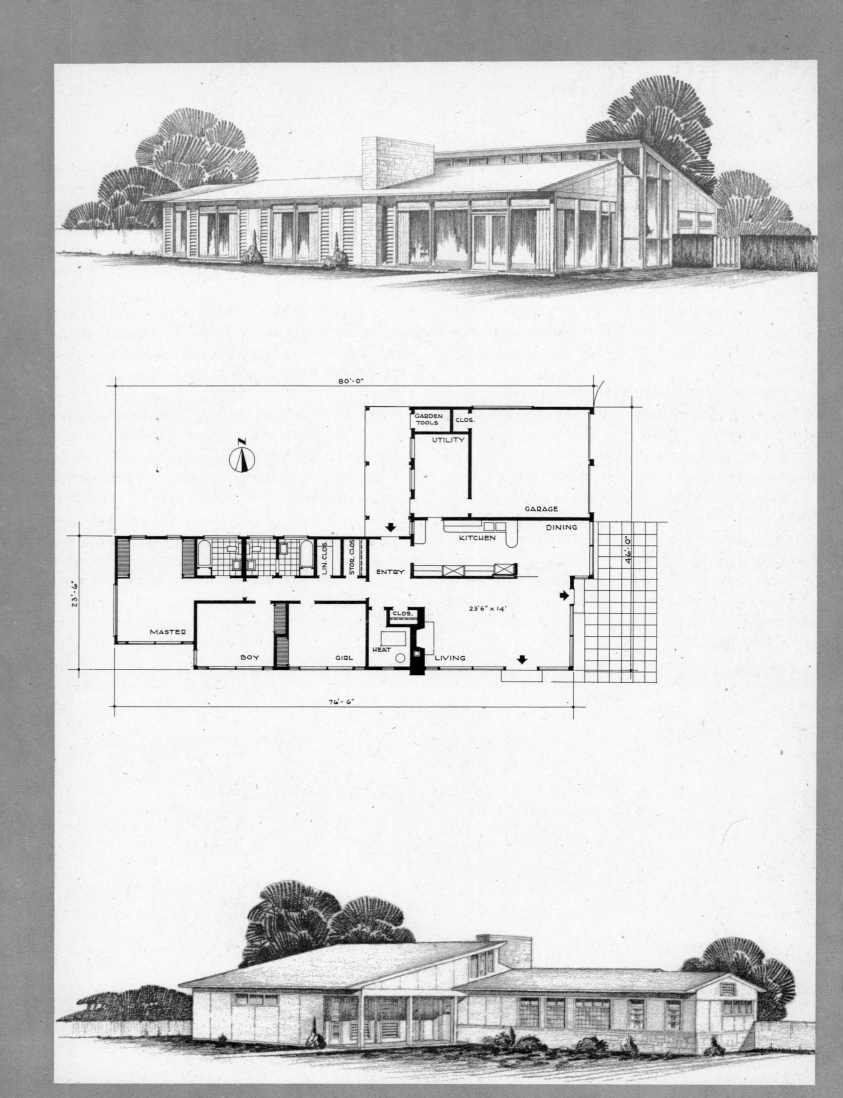

GARDEN
TOOLS   CLOS.

UTILITY

GARAGE

DINING

KITCHEN

LIN. CLOS.

STOR. CLOS.

ENTRY

23'6" x 14'

MASTER

CLOS.

BOY

GIRL

HEAT

LIVING

80'-0"

23'-6"

76'-6"

4'-6"-0"

KANSAS

LORENTZ SCHMIDT
Architect

THIS HOUSE was designed primarily as a home which combines the comforts of modern living with the form traditions of the past. The location of Kansas as the geographic center of the United States determined that the design should not follow the colonial or modern of the East or the Spanish of the Far West, but should encompass, as far as possible, the designs of the pioneers who built what they could with native materials and who lived, worked in, and loved the out-of-doors.

The low, rambling, ranch style recalls the days when Texas cattle, by the hundred thousands, were herded to the new railroads for eastward shipment, and when Abilene, at the end of the Chisholm Trail, was the first of the wild cow towns where Bill Hickok, Bat Masterson, and other straight-shooting law-enforcement officers fought the notorious outlaws of the era.

This plan was developed around the kitchen, in which the average housewife in this part of the country spends so many hours. Easy access to all parts of the house and to the front entrance was the prime requisite, eliminating the necessity of travel through other rooms and reducing the number of steps demanded by the systematic business of operating a home.

A high ceiling and clerestory windows make the kitchen a pleasant room, cool in summer and warm in winter.

Emphasis was placed on the development of pri-vacy within the house. Bedrooms were located in one wing so they could be closed off from the rest of the house. Privacy from the street is obtained by the unusual location of rooms and by the use of translucent glass.

Closets, wardrobe, and storage facilities are provided in such extent that even the most meticulous housewife should have no complaint that there is "no place to put things." There are specially designed wardrobes for each member of the family. Towel cabinets are conveniently located in each bathroom. A large linen closet is provided in the bedroom hall, next to a cedar-lined storage closet which should accommodate all out-of-season clothing of the entire family. There is more storage space in the garage and general storage for trunks and similar articles over the utility room.

The materials used in the construction of the house are, as far as possible, local products, chosen to necessitate a minimum of upkeep.

The site assumed for this house is 125 by 140 feet, with streets on the north and west sides. The house can be adapted, however, to an inside 125-foot lot.

Hedge is planted about the living yard for privacy, and with the large glass expanse of the south wall looking out onto this lawn, the outdoor living so traditional in this region achieves full enjoyment.

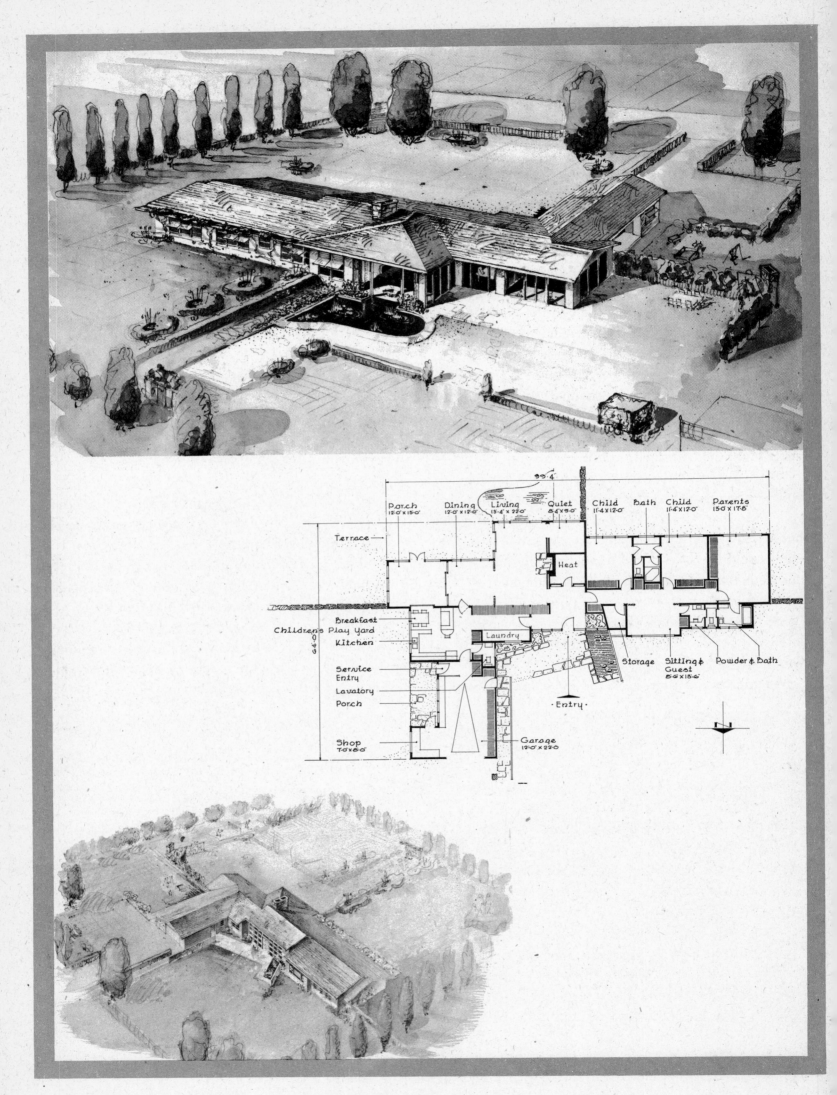

Porch
12'-0" x 15'-0"

Dining
12'-0" x 12'-0"

Living
13'-4" x 22'-0"

Quiet
8'-4" x 8'-0"

Child
11'-4" x 12'-0"

Bath

Child
11'-4" x 12'-0"

Parents
15'-0" x 17'-8"

Terrace

Heat

Breakfast

Children's Play Yard

Kitchen

Laundry

Service Entry

Storage

Sitting & Guest
8'-6" x 15'-6"

Powder & Bath

Lavatory

Porch

Entry

Shop
7'-0" x 8'-0"

Garage
12'-0" x 22'-0"

KENTUCKY

C. JULIAN OBERWARTH
Architect

THE DEVELOPMENT of the Kentucky solar house seeks to recapture some of the charm of early Kentucky home life while giving full attention to modern planning, techniques, and materials, sound construction and economy.

The climate of the Blue Grass State is neither predominantly hot nor predominantly cold. Here nature is a deft wardrobe mistress costuming the four seasons accurately but colorfully for their correctly timed entrance upon the scene. Each brings the thrill and variety

under all conditions; ease of parent supervision of children; variety of possibilities for entertaining guests; adjacent pools and inside planting that add gaiety, freshness, and drama to the fun of living in this house.

The angle of the sun's rays to exterior walls is of utmost importance, and proper use of this knowledge in conjunction with control of the sun by use of overhangs and hermetically sealed double glazing can be advantageous not alone to winter heating but as well to year-round living pleasure and comfort.

that make life so satisfying for Kentuckians—and gracious living is a characteristic of her people that is not confined to any single season.

For a home to achieve distinction in Kentucky it must recognize and satisfy the demands thus made on it. The plan must make it possible literally to transport the whole of a beautiful spring morning right into the house, but must not forget that the rain and fog of a chilly November dawn had better remain outside. It must provide for everyday life—for entertaining, formally and informally; for seclusion and quiet; for riotous fun and confusion.

Details of this house worthy of note include the location of the kitchen in the direct center of living, play, and service areas; the effort to gain a view to the south for all rooms, even breakfast nook and kitchen, without excessive length of plan; provision for quiet and privacy

Since a due-south exposure offers the best both in benefits and control, there remains the problem of how best to handle the plan with relation to east and west exposures. It is apparent that well-insulated west walls with as little glass as possible are desirable. For kitchen, breakfast room, and play areas early-morning summer sun is to be sought, but not the midday or afternoon sun. Dining room and all living areas should have due-south exposure, but in summertime these should be the first to creep into shadow as the sun dips toward the west.

Cross-ventilation for bedrooms is achieved by jalousies at the doors, and windows on the north side.

The reader will not find experimental or radical design in the Kentucky solar house—rather he will find the results of a careful effort to blend the best features of new planning and old into a pattern for happy living.

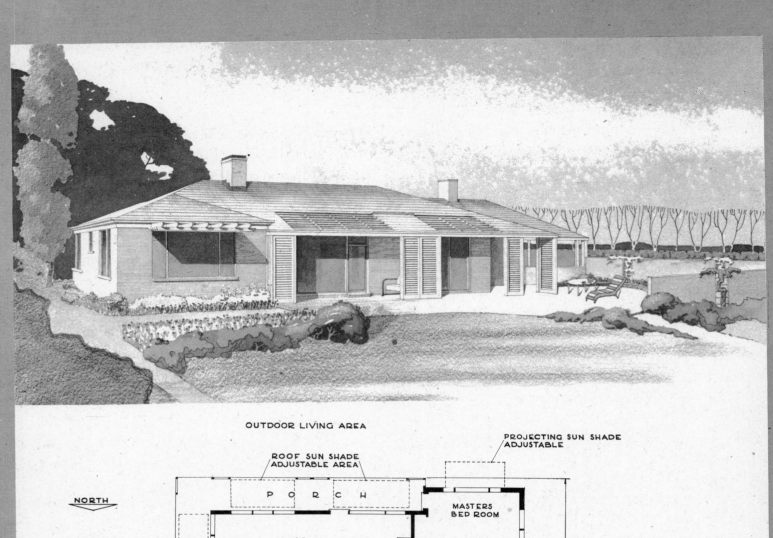

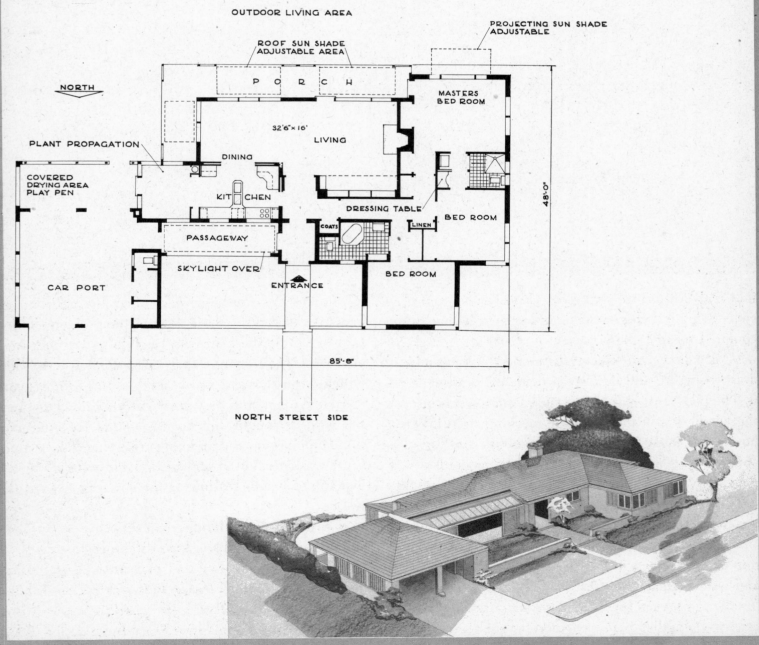

OUTDOOR LIVING AREA

PROJECTING SUN SHADE
ADJUSTABLE

ROOF SUN SHADE
ADJUSTABLE AREA

NORTH

P O R C H

MASTERS
BED ROOM

PLANT PROPAGATION

32'6"×16'

LIVING

COVERED
DRYING AREA
PLAY PEN

DINING

48'-0"

KIT CHEN

DRESSING TABLE

BED ROOM

LINEN

COATS

PASSAGEWAY

SKYLIGHT OVER

CAR PORT

ENTRANCE

BED ROOM

85'-8"

NORTH STREET SIDE

TENNESSEE

J. FRAZER SMITH
Architect

UNLIKE MANY other regions of our country, houses in the South have developed through many generations around the theory of catering to shade rather than to sun. We have, in seeking a flexible house design to meet the demands of modern living, taken full advantage of both.

The design was based on a one-floor arrangement separating the sleeping quarters from the noise of the living areas. The street is on the north side of the lot and the living-dining room and master bedroom face south, looking out onto a sunny garden. The approach by automobile permits the owner to enter directly through the morning room or to bring guests in through a glass-covered passageway to the main front entrance.

From the entrance vestibule every room is accessible without having to pass through any other room. The living-dining room, opposite the vestibule and apart from all interfering traffic lines, achieves thorough privacy. Sliding doors separate the dining section from the kitchen.

A morning room, east of the kitchen, may be used as a breakfast room, greenhouse or laundry, and has in one corner a boiler for heating. When the breakfast table is not in use it may be rolled toward the north wall, to stand over a frozen-food locker.

Just off the morning room is a paved, sheltered area for use as a covered play space for the children, and in the warmer months for general laundry work. Storage space for laundry has been provided just off this area, and there is ample room for garden tools. In this area is a servant's toilet.

A flexible treatment for shielding and admitting sunlight makes use of adjustable sunshades, roof louvers, and jalousies. The radiant heating system divides the house into two zones controlled by separate thermostats. The three rooms on the south side are on one circuit, enabling the occupants to take advantage of the heat furnished by the sun, without uncomfortable, unnecessary temperature lags.

The living and morning rooms open onto a private terrace on the garden front, and a walk leads around a wide expanse of lawn to a barbecue grill.

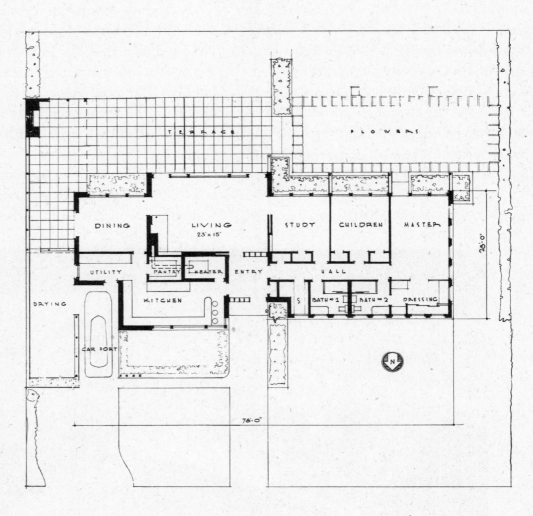

DINING LIVING
23'x15' STUDY CHILDREN MASTER

TERRACE FLOWERS

UTILITY PANTRY HEATER ENTRY HALL

DRYING KITCHEN BATH N°1 BATH N°2 DRESSING

CAR PORT

78'-0"

28'-0"

ALABAMA

CLYDE C. PEARSON
Architect

IN PLANNING the Alabama solar house we have assumed that it will stand on a lot 100 feet wide and 150 feet deep, with the street on the north, and that it will be occupied by a family of four—father, mother, two small children. The lot, orientation, and family determined the plan. The entire lot was planned as a unit, with the house itself the part that provides shelter.

The house is divided into living and sleeping areas, which are tied together by the entry. This creates two zones for heating and ventilating. The living area consists of the large living room and dining space separated from it by the fireplace wall. These rooms flow into each other, and with large glass areas extending down to the floor they become a part of the terrace and yard. Next to the dining area is a pergola and barbecue pit. The terrace and pergola are only a part of the over-all yard development, which embraces a large lawn area, flower garden, badminton court, and small vegetable garden.

The sleeping wing consists of the master bedroom, children's bedroom, and guest bedroom or study. It was assumed that the two children are small and may use the same bedroom for a few years, after which time the guest room may be converted for one of them. This extra room, if used as a study, may become an integral part of the living room by sliding the connecting door into its concealed pocket.

The spacious master bedroom has three exposures and achieves full cross-ventilation through the adjacent dressing alcove. The alcove houses large closets with sliding doors and built-in chests of drawers. A door from the bedroom gives direct passage to the flower garden.

The kitchen is placed and planned to enable the housewife to carry on her work with a minimum of effort. A pantry separates the kitchen and dining area. A breakfast bar offers room for four and takes a mini-

mum of space. The kitchen cabinets have sliding glass doors. A utility room houses the laundry. The service entrance is through the carport and utility room, providing a quick passage to the drying yard and serving as a delivery entrance and bad-weather entrance.

Normally, in designing solar houses, the roof overhang is calculated against the position of the sun on December 21, its lowest point, and on June 21, when it is at its zenith. Since August is usually the hottest month

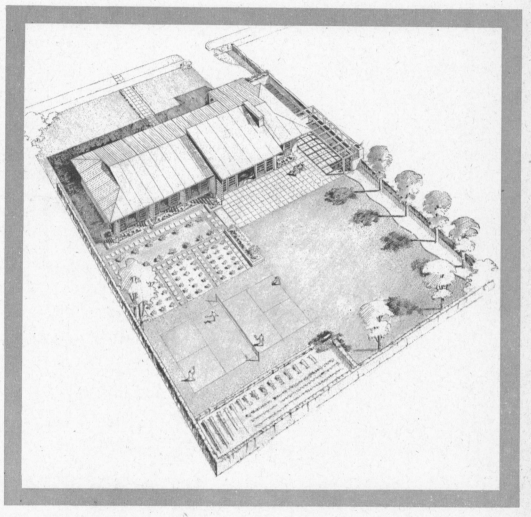

in Alabama, however, the overhang of this house is calculated to interdict the rays of the sun at noon on August 21.

Under the windows are louvers which allow ventilation and circulation of air while the windows are closed. The louvers are opened and closed by sliding panels. To keep out the low afternoon sun when desired we have provided vertical side louver slats for each south-facing room. These do not block the breeze, but simply act as a shield from the sun.

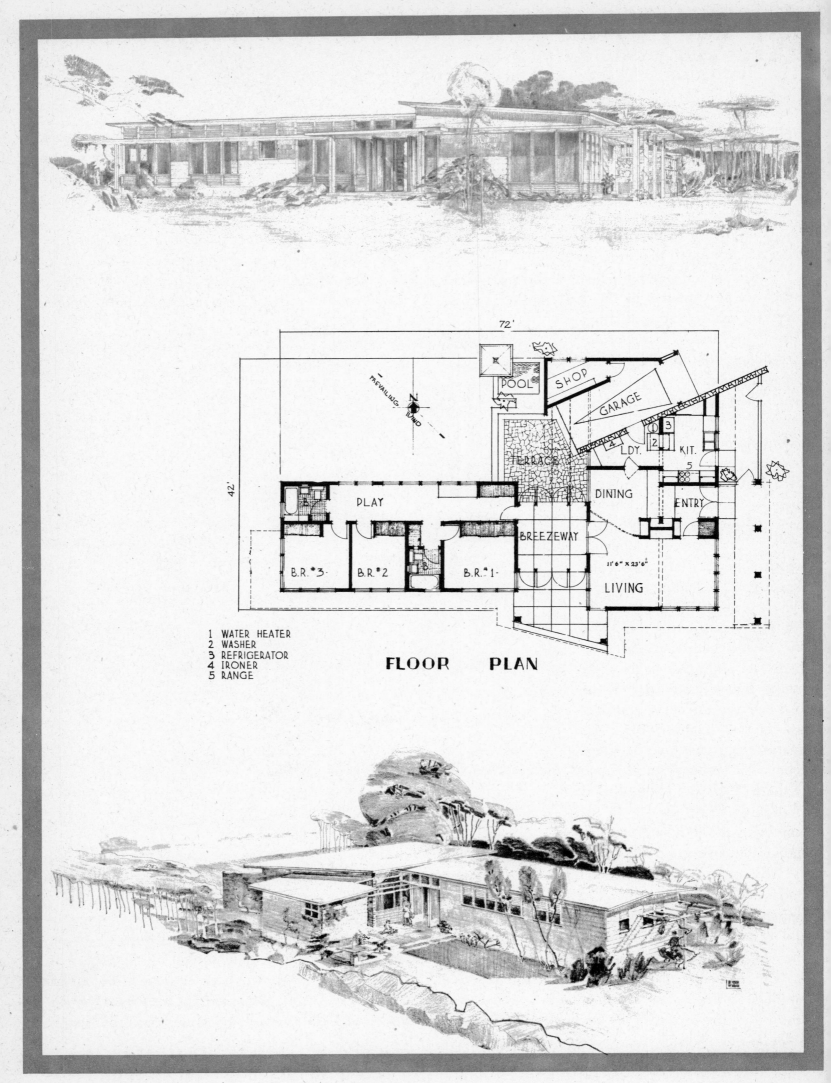

FLOOR PLAN

72'

42'

PREVAILING WIND

N

POOL

SHOP

GARAGE

TERRACE

LDY.

KIT.

4

2

3

5

DINING

ENTRY

PLAY

BREEZEWAY

B.R. *3*

B.R. *2*

B.R. *1*

11'6" X 23'6"

LIVING

1 WATER HEATER
2 WASHER
3 REFRIGERATOR
4 IRONER
5 RANGE

MISSISSIPPI

EDGAR L. MALVANEY
Architect

BUILT almost entirely of native materials and supplies processed near at hand, this solar house will be suitable to almost any one of Mississippi's historic regions, whether it be the Delta, with its wide, flat fields and rich plantation lands, the Natchez District, still ornamented by the manor houses of the old South, or the new industrialism of the Black Prairie, west of the Tennessee hills.

Its hand-rived cypress shingles of silver gray, its parasols, columns, and trim in cream, its light-blue soffit of the eaves, will give the house a happy, comfortable, and hospitable aspect in keeping with its Southern environment.

This solar house was designed with two extremes of temperature in mind. In summer in the deep South, on the occasions when the mercury soars to the 100-degree mark, the greatest possible amount of natural ventilation and protection from the sun's rays is essential. In the winter the temperature sometimes falls to 10 or 12 degrees, making hearty invitation to solar warmth a wise expression.

These plans provide a livable, convenient, and attractive house that will meet these two extremes.

A central breezeway, which is really a large entrance hall opening through double doors onto a rear terrace at the north and onto the main entry at the south, is a central feature of the house. The structure is planned as two rectangles joined together by the breezeway to form an "L." One rectangle contains the three bedrooms, and two baths, backed by a play area which is in effect the corridor to the bedrooms. It faces lengthwise to the south, giving the three bedrooms an open face in the direction of the sun. The other rectangle contains the living-dining room, fronting on the south, backed by the main entrance, which faces east, the kitchen, and the laundry. Opening as it does into the play area and into the living room, the breezeway provides full circulation of air from complete north-south ventilation.

Placed diagonally to the rear of the kitchen, the garage offers direct access for the family car by means of a driveway slanting from the street.

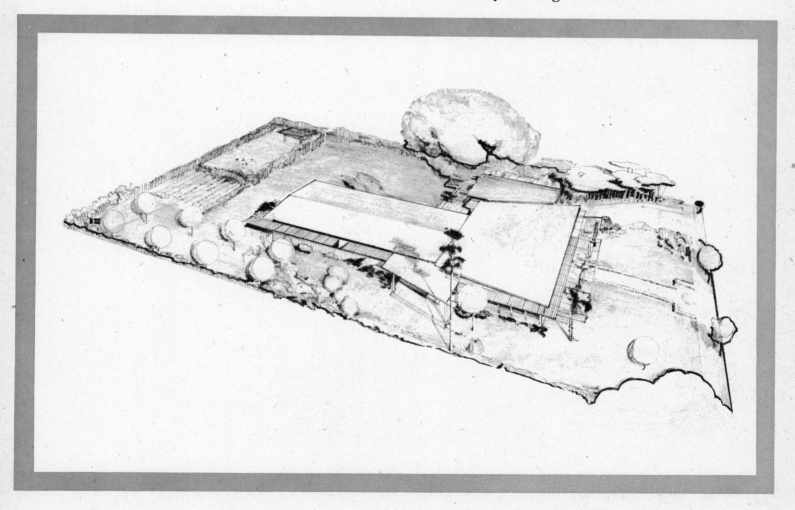

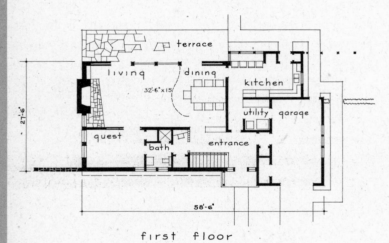

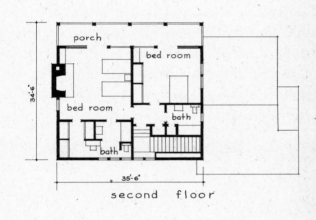

first floor

second floor

96

ARKANSAS

H. RAY BURKS
Architect

ALTHOUGH startling scientific discoveries will have terrific impact on our way of living, it will take more energy than the split atom generates to change people's tastes and desires in the planning of their homes. Regardless of doctrines advanced by theorists, we will not strip our abodes down to the bare essentials of basic forms, and this refusal is by no means a sign of enslavement to the past.

north. The porch and terrace are at the south, as are the living room, dining room, kitchen, and two bedrooms. The living-dining rooms open onto the garden through two sliding Thermopane panels. The southern exposure for the kitchen gains sunlight and a view for those charged with the chores in the room that is usually the control cabin of a house.

The less important quarters, such as the garage, en-

This state ranges from flatlands to the sharply rising Ouachitas and Ozarks, from cotton fields of the plantation country near the Mississippi to grazing land along the Texas line. Its demeanor is a combination of the South's quiet courtesy and the open-handed friendliness of the West. Its people are tradesmen or miners or farmers or cotton planters or stockmen in broadbrimmed Stetsons or hill men whose ancestors homesteaded the territory. The overwhelming majority of these men and their families prefer a home designed along traditional lines.

In this solar house, using native materials, we have developed an exterior style reminiscent of early American architecture. The open plan has been used without sacrificing privacy.

The Arkansas house is designed for an inside lot approximately 100 feet wide. The street side is to the

trance, guest room, bath, and stairway, are placed on the street side with few windows, as a screen for privacy and against the hostile elements of weather from the north.

The north-side windows are purposely small, to reduce heat loss, and are double-glazed. In the summer these windows can be closed when the attic fan is in operation, to prevent ingress of street dust.

The flagstone hearth of the living room is recalled again in the terrace, which is an extension of the living area. The garden is screened from the drying yard on the west by a fence and hedge. The view of the garden from within the house creates a feeling of infinite spaciousness. Strategic placement of plate-glass mirrors will enhance this feeling by reflecting scenes as well as light. The use of large glass areas makes it possible to unfold the entire panorama of the south garden.

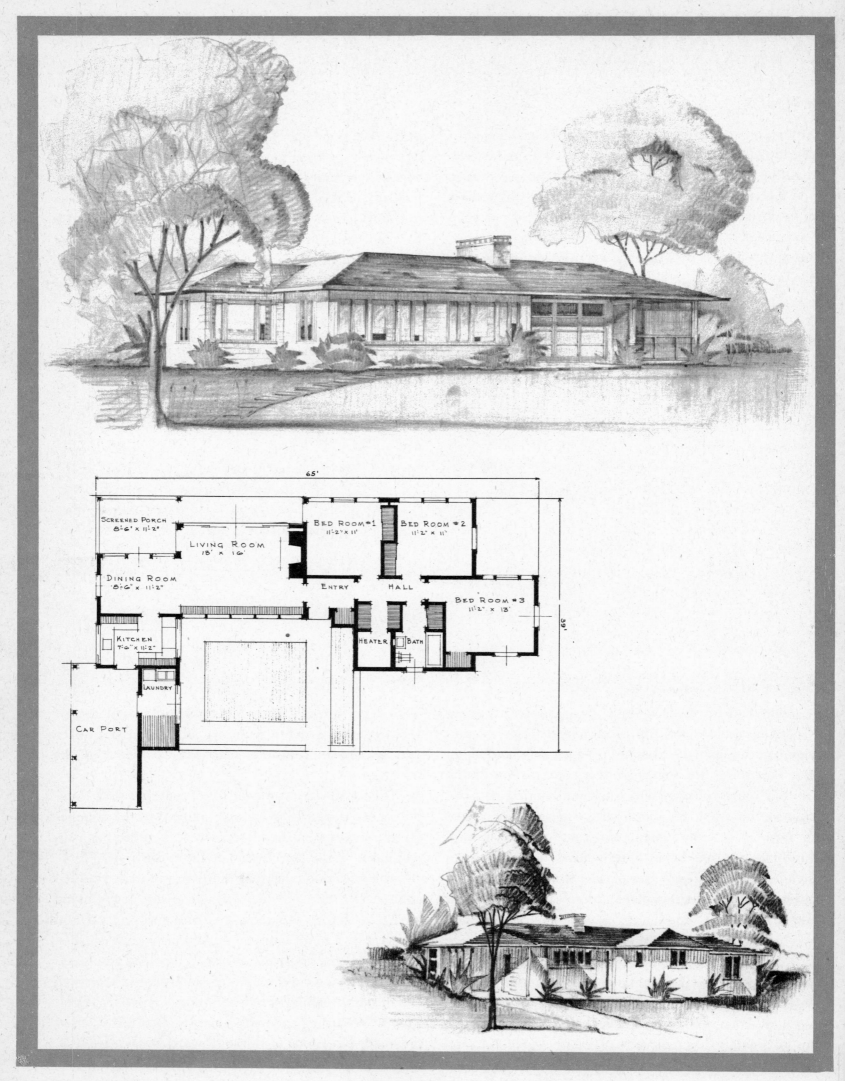

SCREENED PORCH
8'-6" x 11'-2"

LIVING ROOM
18' x 16'

BED ROOM #1
11'-2" x 11'

BED ROOM #2
11'-2" x 11'

DINING ROOM
8'-6" x 11'-2"

ENTRY

HALL

BED ROOM #3
11'-2" x 13'

KITCHEN
7'-6" x 11'-2"

HEATER

BATH

LAUNDRY

CAR PORT

65'

39'

LOUISIANA

RICHARD KOCH
Architect

THE PRINCIPLES which are basic in what today is known as solar housing are not new to the South; the development of the idea in Louisiana is the history of the early architecture of the state, a style borrowed largely from the West Indies.

During the hot summers, the rooms of a house must be protected from the sun and from frequent showers. This problem was solved by porches on four sides of plantation houses and in New Orleans by covered balconies on the streets. In winter the porches did not cut off the low rays of the sun, which gave heat and light to the building interiors.

The problem of today's solar house is the use of modern materials and an arrangement of rooms suitable to modern living. This has developed a new type of house, as modern heating and insulation do not require high ceilings and picturesque roofs and chimneys.

Selected for the Louisiana solar house is a lot 100 by 120 feet in a subdivision on the lake front of New Orleans. There is a street to the north; the east faces a boulevard and park with large oaks; on the west is a neighbor's dwelling, and to the south is a shaded lane to be used only by pedestrians.

Naturally, the living portions of the house should face the south, as the prevailing breezes in summer are from that direction and the planting and trees on the boundaries of the lane would give a maximum of privacy. The entrance will be from the north, and the service from the east. As the terrain in this neighborhood is flat, views are created by the division of the lot into pleasingly shaped areas with a background of evergreen trees.

As seen from the garden, the house shows a long, low roof line with a wide overhang, and broken by a large brick chimney. The walls of the sleeping rooms facing south are of glass and are partly movable. The living room, off a small porch, has sliding glass doors so that one easily steps out onto the terrace. At the far end is the screened-in porch, carrying out the lines of the sleeping room.

The living room, the link between the service and the sleeping quarters, has high windows in the north wall, underneath which are bookcases and storage for magazines and games. The south side facing the enclosed garden is a wall of Thermopane. A screened porch, a necessity in this warm climate, fills in the corner of the house and would be used nine months of the year.

Each bedroom, facing south and southwest, has two exposures with cross-ventilation, and the southwest bedroom is virtually a sleeping porch. The kitchen is entered from the carport, as also are the laundry and storage room. A small service yard closed from the street by a fence and heavy shrubbery is sufficient for the activities of the kitchen.

The garden to the rear of the house centers on the terrace off the living room. A walk from the gate at the lane through the flower garden carries past the terrace to the informal paved area under the large tree at the southwest corner of the property, forming an oval-shaped lawn. A view of the living end of the house shows the living room's large Thermopane doors opening out onto the terrace, where the informal planting and comfortable chairs give an intimate character that modern living calls for.

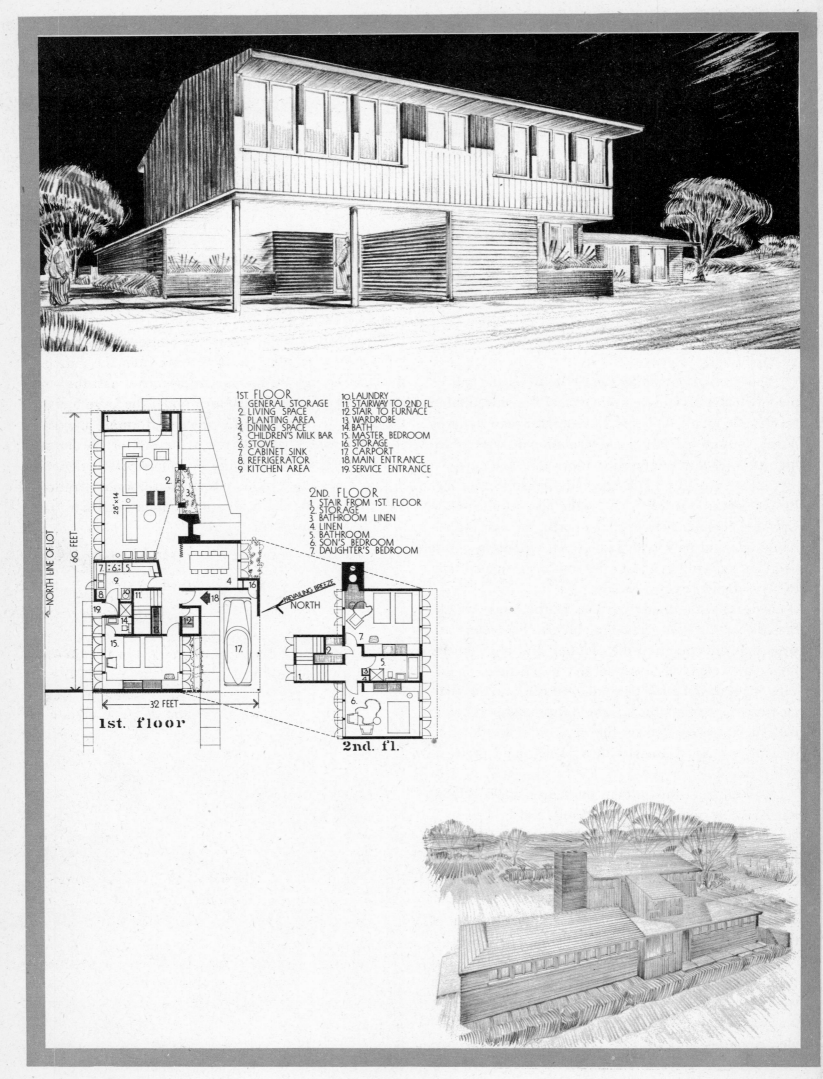

1ST. FLOOR
1. GENERAL STORAGE
2. LIVING SPACE
3. PLANTING AREA
4. DINING SPACE
5. CHILDREN'S MILK BAR
6. STOVE
7. CABINET SINK
8. REFRIGERATOR
9. KITCHEN AREA
10. LAUNDRY
11. STAIRWAY TO 2ND. FL.
12. STAIR TO FURNACE
13. WARDROBE
14. BATH
15. MASTER BEDROOM
16. STORAGE
17. CARPORT
18. MAIN ENTRANCE
19. SERVICE ENTRANCE

2ND. FLOOR
1. STAIR FROM 1ST. FLOOR
2. STORAGE
3. BATHROOM LINEN
4. LINEN
5. BATHROOM
6. SON'S BEDROOM
7. DAUGHTER'S BEDROOM

NORTH LINE OF LOT
60 FEET
28'x14
32 FEET

1st. floor

PREVAILING BREEZE
NORTH

2nd. fl.

100

OKLAHOMA

HENRY L. KAMPHOEFNER
Architect[*]

The Oklahoma solar house has been designed for an inside lot 100 feet wide by 150 feet deep, and fronting on the east side of an urban street. Houses on this type of plot are often planned so badly that the specified lot offers a challenge to the designer.

This house has been placed close to the street and to the north lot line, but the design has been worked out carefully to screen the house in those two directions. There are no windows on the east or west sides. The plan opens well to the south and the side and rear of the lot, for maximum privacy and view across the lawn.

The house was designed for relaxed, informal living. The main-entrance vestibule serves as a pivot point off which all rooms work, and passage to or from any room is possible without disturbing any other part of the house. The living-dining area may open into a single unified space when the occasion demands. The storage wall is used throughout the house, and ample, strategically placed storage spaces are provided.

Since the climate here is mild and most rains come from the north and east, the carport is brought into the house but left open on the west and south. Visitors arriving by automobile may enter the house under cover.

Exterior finishes are common brick and redwood siding. The pitched roofs are red-cedar shingles, and the flat roofs are tar and gravel. Interior finishes are chiefly of plywoods with plaster ceilings and hardwood floors. Simple fabrics will be used to screen the windows at night.

Glass is used freely in the exterior walls, but in large amounts only where it can be protected from the summer sun and in no area where the family's privacy will be violated. Translucent-glass louvers are used to screen the lower bedroom windows from view while admitting light and air.

Planting is an integral part of the architecture as used in the areas next to the house and throughout the plot. It screens and softens specific areas, and enriches space.

[*]Perspectives by: Nat Baker and John H. Lattimore

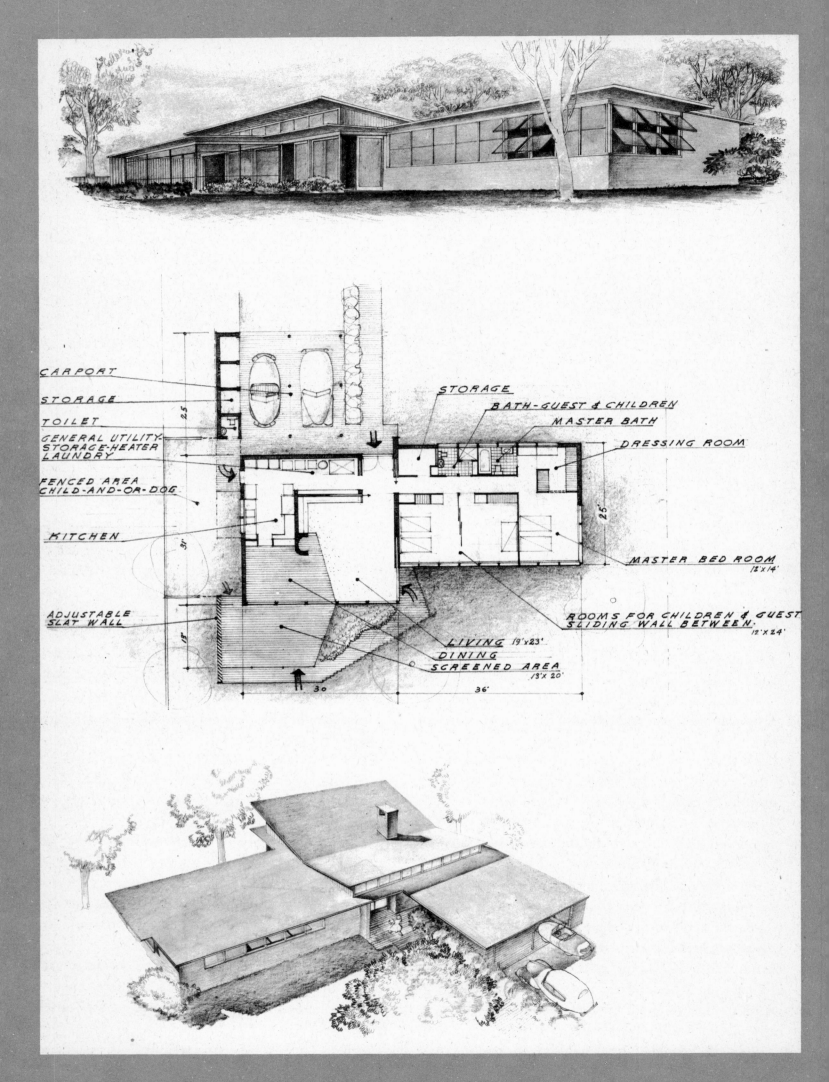

CARPORT

STORAGE

TOILET

GENERAL UTILITY-
STORAGE-HEATER
LAUNDRY

FENCED AREA
CHILD-AND-OR-DOG

KITCHEN

ADJUSTABLE
SLAT WALL

STORAGE

BATH-GUEST & CHILDREN

MASTER BATH

DRESSING ROOM

MASTER BED ROOM
12'X14'

ROOMS FOR CHILDREN & GUEST
SLIDING WALL BETWEEN
12'X24'

LIVING 19'X23'
DINING
SCREENED AREA
13'X20'

25'

31'

13'

30'

36'

25'

102

TEXAS

O'NEIL FORD
Architect

TEXAS IS BIG and its extremes are great both in climate and variety of topography. An eight-hundred-mile line may be drawn within its borders and its northwest plains may be snow-covered while citrus trees bloom in its Rio Grande Valley. In the forested northeast area the altitude ranges near 300 feet above sea level; in the far southwest peaks rise above 8000 feet among arid stretches of brush and cactus. Almost all of it is generally known as "hot country," but no house that would sit down on the treeless plains of the Panhandle would fit in the valley of the Rio Grande.

This house is planned for the middle area, somewhere between Dallas and San Antonio, but with slight changes in orientation and fenestration, and use of planting, it would serve well in any section of the state.

There are only a few months in winter when a Texan may be persuaded to give heating a paramount place in his house planning. The most persistent enemy is the sun, and the most cherished friend is the prevailing summer breeze.

Because of structural limitations, the early, indigenous southwestern shelters were built with thick walls and small windows to keep the sun out. This Texas house is so designed that well-insulated walls keep out the heat and good ventilation and views are provided by many large windows adequately protected by wide roof overhangs. These roof extensions provide shelter from the sun except in the brief Texas winters when sunlight is welcome in the home. The windows can remain open in all but the hardest-blowing rains. The principle is not new to the southwest. The cowhand's ten-gallon hat, the Mexican's sombrero, are portable overhangs.

This house is planned for easy management with or without domestic help. The entry provides ready access to the bedroom wing, the service area, or the living areas. The living-dining space, the screened porch, and the garden (separated from the living area by landscaping for privacy as well as pleasant vistas) are set apart from one another only by flexible partitions.

The master bedroom has a dressing area and a private bath. The children's rooms are planned for the utmost flexibility, with a sliding partition making it possible to provide a large play space, bedroom-playroom, or two smaller rooms, when an occasional guest arrives.

A shady place in the breeze is not only desirable but necessary if you want to sit outside on summer afternoons. This house has a porch which not only is a shade within itself but also serves to shade the lawn to its east. In this locality glare is a serious problem, and the porch will go far toward relieving it in the living-dining area. You will understand why Texans take the brightness of their sun so seriously when you realize that Texas is in the latitude of the northern Sahara.

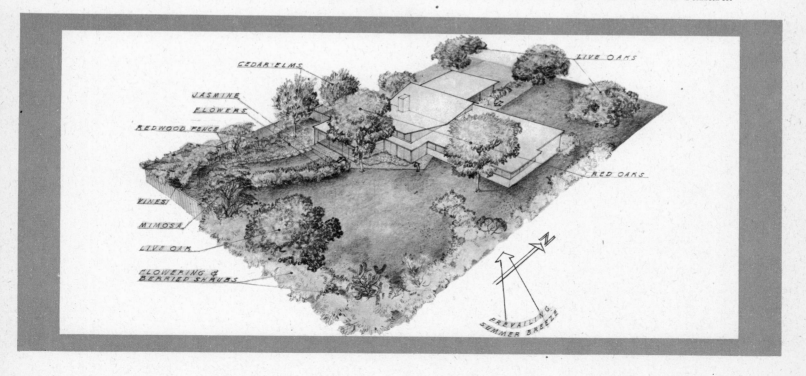

MONTANA

RALPH H. CUSHING
Architect

IN THIS SOLAR HOUSE we have sought to provide a compact, comfortable, well-constructed, well-insulated home at a minimum of cost and with a maximum of space. It is simple in plan, free of tricks and gadgets, in the tradition of the self-reliant West.

Entry is through a covered porch into a vestibule which forms the hub of the house. From this central core the living-dining room, kitchen, lavatory, recreation room, and garage are immediately accessible. All main rooms invite the rays of the sun. Screened, louvered intakes near the floor in all rooms bring in fresh air and leave the window surfaces unencumbered. To provide seclusion there are no windows except the garage windows on the east and west property lines.

The living-dining area is placed on a private court, with a brick wall windbreak blending interior and exterior and carrying into a fireplace.

The kitchen, planned for a house without a maid, is placed centrally to the north, where it is cool in summer and has ample constant light. The room is equipped with a pull-down snack table, a ventilating fan, and a clothes chute.

It was felt that a well-lighted basement with ample facilities for many purposes was more sensible than the sacrifice of desirable lawn area to provide a ground-floor utility room, which is usually inadequate.

The local climate is such that while daytime may be warm in the summer, nights are invariably cool. This dictates the use of the small attic space for a ventilating system in which a fan draws the cool evening air through the house and forces out the warm attic air. This system, with well-insulated walls and ceilings, will provide a most comfortable house.

The bedrooms are isolated from the center of activity and are reached through a hall covered with knotty pine. The hall is lighted by a bank of large windows above a flower box, and is amply equipped with closet space and clothes chutes.

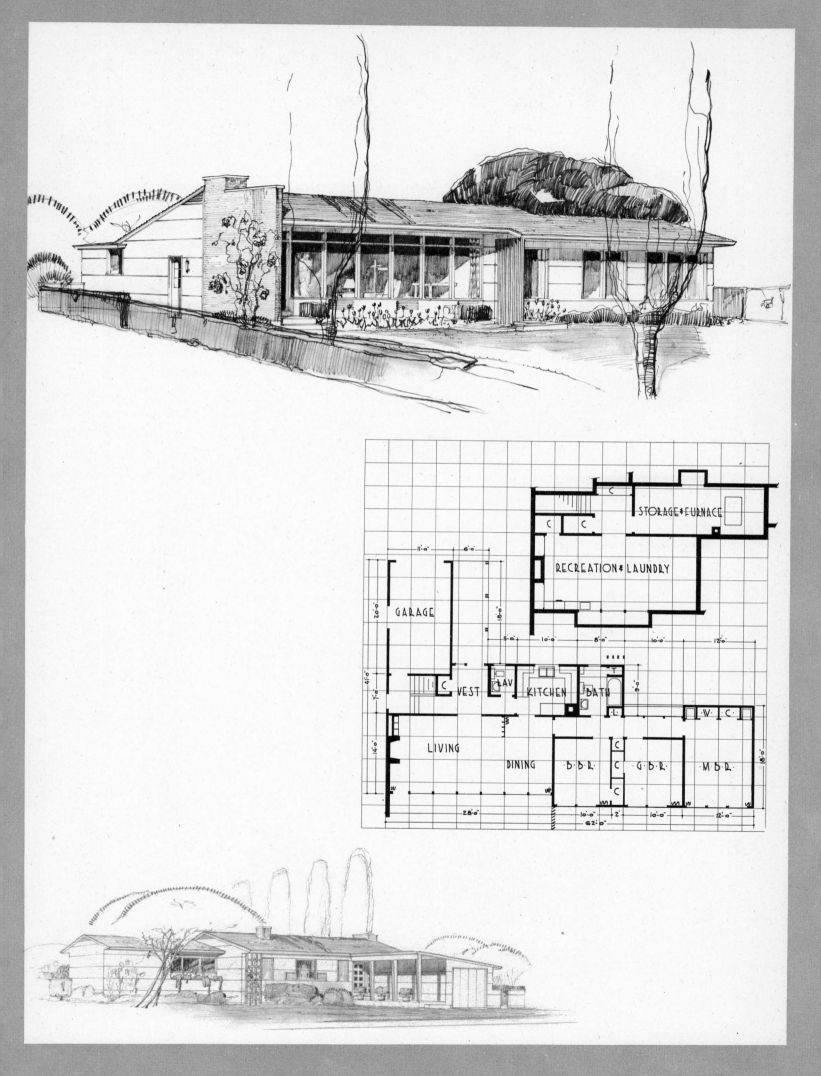

GARAGE

STORAGE & FURNACE

RECREATION & LAUNDRY

VEST

LAV

KITCHEN

BATH

LIVING

DINING

B.B.R.

G.B.R.

M.B.R.

GARAGE

LAUNDRY   STORAGE

PORCH

KITCHEN

5'4"

HALL   CLOS.   LINEN   BATH   BATH   CLOS.   CLOS.

HEATER
ROOM

DINING ROOM

LIVING ROOM
19'6"X 15'

CLOSET   CLOSET   MASTER
BED ROOM

SON'S
ROOM   DAUGHTER'S
ROOM

TERRACE

69'

WYOMING

FREDERIC HUTCHINSON PORTER
Architect

IN DESIGNING a home which would be adaptable by Wyoming and suitable in style and arrangement to the region, many factors demand consideration, among them topography, weather, scenery, and the predilection of the people for outdoor living.

Wyoming is a land of many mountains and vast areas of treeless plains, of verdant river valleys and irrigated tracts, of open landscape and long vistas of range country, of clear, bright skies, of northwest winds that in winter may be extremely disagreeable.

In these plans the western ranch-house style is adapted to the many full days of sunshine that prevail in Wyoming. The orientation is such as to allow some sunlight to strike at all sides of the rectangle at some time during the day; most Wyoming townsites are laid out with building lots at this angle. Shelter must be provided against the prevailing northwesterly winds, and for that reason the principal exposure is usually to the east and south, as is the case in this plan.

The one-story plan is much preferred in a region where outdoor living is so much the rule. The principal rooms of this house face the south, and the service wing forms an "L" to shield the entrance court from the winter winds.

Across the south face are arrayed, from west to east, the dining room, the living room, two bedrooms for children, and the master bedroom. The dining room, opening onto a dining terrace, has three exposures. The living room, with built-in bookcases, an under-window cabinet, and a stone fireplace, has two, as do the master bedroom and the child's bedroom adjoining it.

The grounds are planted to welcome the sunshine on the south, while a minimum of planting on the north keeps the light snowfalls from drifting across walks or driveways.

The long, horizontal lines have been accented in keeping with the level distances of the plains, while the large chimney has been built of native stone recalling the rocky mountain slopes.

The general composition will blend with the Wyoming landscape better than almost any other style.

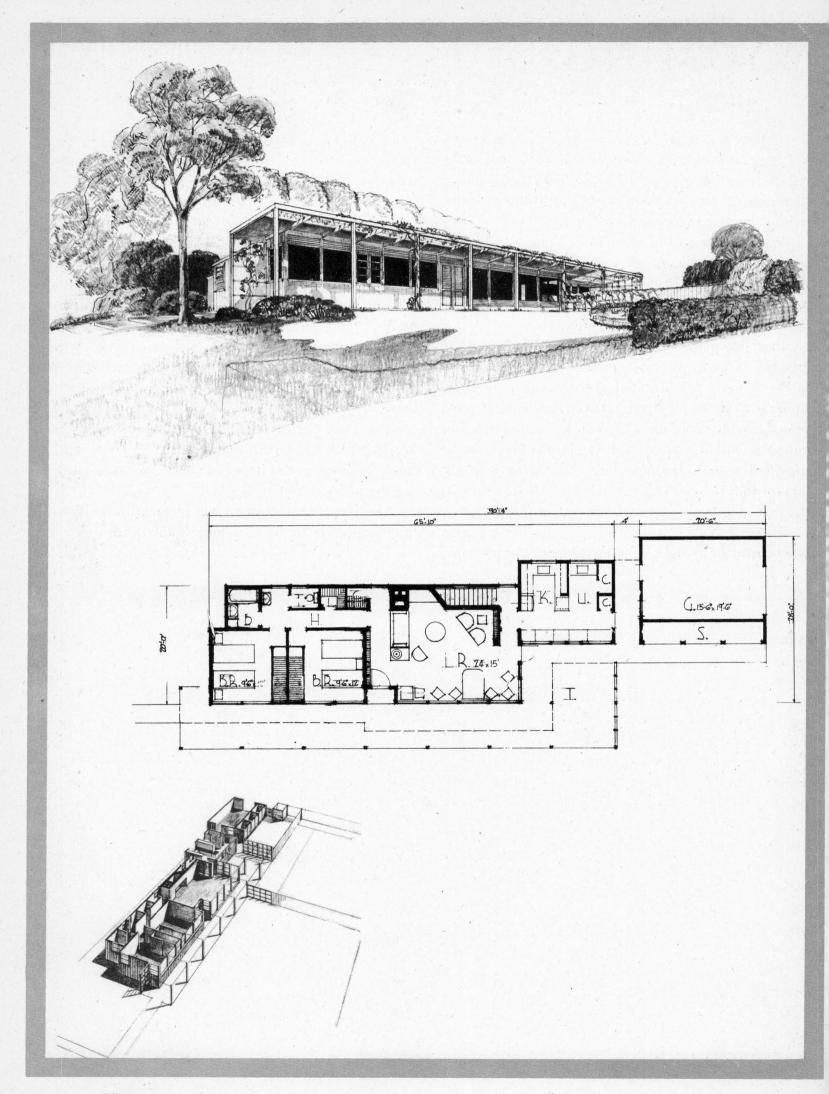

COLORADO

BURNHAM HOYT
Architect

To TAKE the fullest advantage of solar heating, as many rooms as possible in this plan have southern exposure. These rooms are arranged along a narrow south porch which runs the full length to the terrace at the east.

We prefer to think of this porch as a Spanish-American *portal*. Borrowed from New Mexico and the southwest, this feature provides an outdoor living area that is attractive and comfortable, and usable almost every day, thanks to the year-round sunshine of Colorado.

In order to preserve as much space as possible for sunlight on the south, the house has been planned only one room deep, and is placed as close to the north line of the lot as the building code will allow.

Every principal room has south exposure with fixed Thermopane windows the full width of the room. There are screened transoms for ventilation above the Thermopane panels and, in addition, in the living room, screened adjustable louvers at the floor. There are two or more double-hung windows in each room to insure adequate change of air.

These south windows are protected from the summer sun by the roof of the south porch. Beyond the solid area of the porch roof the rafters have been extended to form a trellis.

The exterior of the Colorado house is of stained pine except for the soffit of the porch, which is painted. Doors and sash are painted or stained, as preferred. Lattices and fences are stained. Brickwork at the interior north wall of the living room is left exposed.

Providing, as it does, shade and view for residents of the solar house, planting is specified in detail as an actual part of the house plan. In addition to a north buffer of evergreens, similar buffers have been indicated along the service alley at the east and on the south party line.

Locust trees will provide shade in the summer and, if trimmed to remove the lower branches, will permit the winter sun to reach the bedroom windows. Grapevines will be planted at the porch posts, and a special flowering vine is planned for the center of the outdoor living space off the living room and kitchen.

The vines on the porch trellis, with their leafing out as summer comes in, provide more and more shade, and, by shedding their leaves with the approach of autumn and winter, give progressively less shade.

A transverse fence cuts off the east portion of the south yard to create a private garden as part of the out-of-door living space.

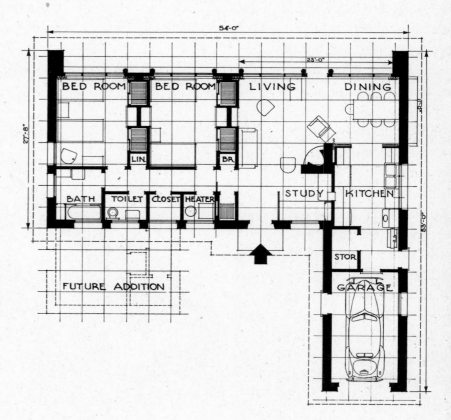

BED ROOM
BED ROOM
LIVING
DINING
LIN.
BR.
BATH TOILET CLOSET HEATER
STUDY
KITCHEN
FUTURE ADDITION
STOR.
GARAGE

54'-0"
23'-0"
27'-8"
53'-0"

NEW MEXICO

JOHN GAW MEEM
Architect

IN THIS LAND of plains, deserts, lofty mountains, buttes, and mesas, the open vistas of the solar house afford its occupants a happy identification with the vast, limitless spaces, the immense distances, the clear air, and the brilliant sunshine which characterize New Mexico.

This house makes ample use of available local materials. From early times, houses in our state have been built of adobe and the pine and cedar logs of near-by forests. By projecting the roof on all four sides, the adobe walls are guarded against erosion and may be plastered with adobe clay, providing a long-lasting surface of earth color which is beautiful and inexpensive. Earth walls are good insulators against both temperature and sound.

The plan is for a family consisting of parents and two young children. As the children grow older they will require separate rooms, for which a future addition is shown in dotted lines.

The house is designed for a lot 75 feet wide by 125 feet deep. It is set back sufficiently from the street to minimize traffic noises and still leave ample room for gardens in the rear, planted to provide maximum privacy. The living-room windows open onto a neat, informal garden, while a fence of cedar posts marks off an area in which the children may romp.

The study alcove provides a comfortable retreat, or an office for the housewife, or sleeping quarters for a guest.

The fireplace, beehive in shape and burning wood vertically, is traditional in design and highly efficient in operation. The design about the opening is in natural-earth pigment. The pine rafter and pine ceiling boards are unfinished and become increasingly beautiful with age.

Decorative patterned glass is utilized effectively for kitchen doors, main entrance screen, and bath enclosure; floors are of concrete covered with asphalt tile, and local flagstone is used for the terrace.

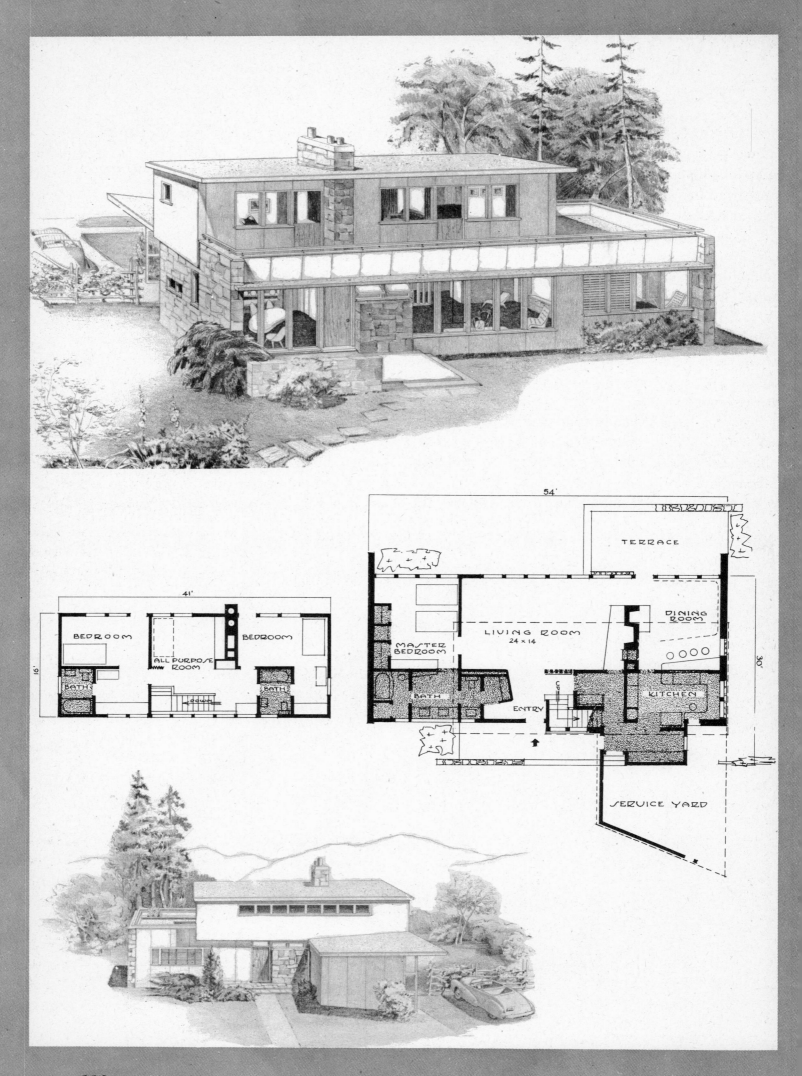

BEDROOM

BEDROOM

ALL PURPOSE ROOM

BATH

BATH

down

41'

16'

54'

TERRACE

LIVING ROOM 24 x 14

DINING ROOM

MASTER BEDROOM

BATH

ENTRY

KITCHEN

SERVICE YARD

30'

IDAHO

THEODORE JAN PRICHARD
Architect

To GENERALIZE about Idaho is folly; only a rash man would attempt it. It is a land of contradictions. Its 83,-557 square miles make it twelfth in area among the forty-eight states; its population, 524,873 by 1940 count, places it forty-third in census rank. Its citizens have no cause for claustrophobia or misanthropy; there is a flavor of openhanded and openhearted hospitality akin to pioneer days.

To build a model home for Idaho likewise is folly.

Her mountains, lakes, woods, canyons, deserts, and rolling wheatfields are as varied as Washington, Oregon, and California together, and as far apart. Therefore, I have taken our own locale in Moscow, Idaho, and a family which, if a bit composite, is yet real, and have tried to build a home for it.

This is a little more house than they can afford; it always is. But if I know the breed, the mortgage will be retired long before it falls due.

The children, like all Idaho children, are self-reliant. Their mother often helps out at the store, at least until school lets out in the afternoon. There is no great reason why she should, except that she did when they first started out, and she likes to do it now. She can work or stay home as she pleases. There are no regular servants in the house. A helper may come in by the hour or the day if the family is lucky enough to get her. If there are guests, the master of the house doesn't mind lending a hand in the kitchen after they've gone.

These are important factors in this design. The children have their own world in the deckhouse. The all-purpose room will serve various needs. It will take care of a nurse if there is illness. It will house an overnight guest. It will be a retreat for some of the family when others are entertaining.

A too-open house is not practical here; the air cools rapidly when the sun goes down; the evenings, even in summer, are usually cool and sometimes downright cold. There is a good deal of dust in the air in the plowing seasons, or when the wind blows; the nights require wool blankets the year around. A little heat from September to June is necessary; December and January are rugged. The summer supper hour, however, can be wonderful, and a dining terrace, if not too shaded, is most useful.

As to style, Idaho is still on the conservative side. Investment of capital is a real concern, and while the individual will show a certain desire for the experimental, pioneer prudence usually wins out. For this reason a number of people interested in building were encouraged to express themselves on this matter. A fairly conservative house was the result—one, however, that would be livable. The materials are Idaho or Western. North Idaho is largely timberland. The rock is native and undressed.

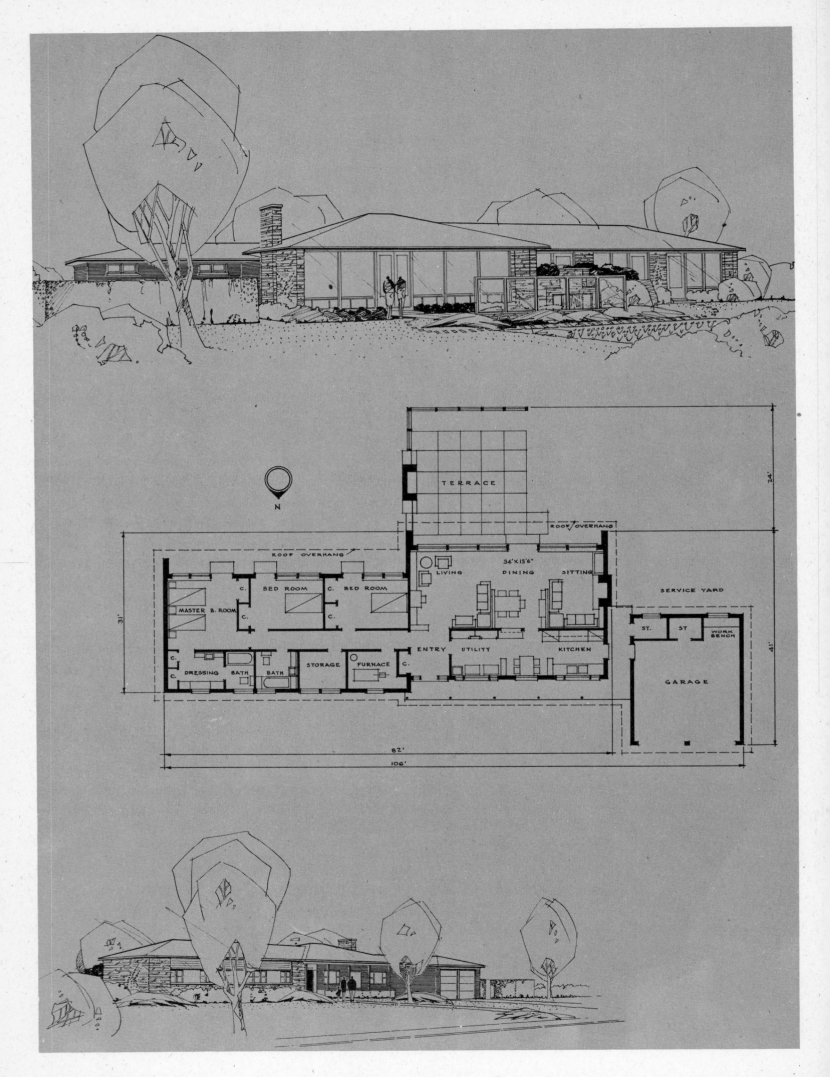

TERRACE

ROOF OVERHANG

ROOF OVERHANG

N

LIVING   DINING   SITTING

34'X13'6"

MASTER B. ROOM

C.   BED ROOM   C.   BED ROOM

C.   C.

C.

SERVICE YARD

ST.   ST   WORK BENCH

C.   DRESSING   BATH   BATH   STORAGE   FURNACE   C.

ENTRY   UTILITY   KITCHEN

GARAGE

31'

41'

24'

82'

106'

UTAH

LOWELL E. PARRISH
Architect

THE PEOPLE of Utah are conservative in their tastes in homes. Generally they do not like the bizarre or the obscure. This solar house, except for the south elevation, has an exterior appearance at little variance with other houses in the region. It also is planned for a state of valleys, mountains, canyons, and desert, with extreme variations of weather in the cycle of the four seasons.

The Utah solar house is composed of four rectangular shapes:

Kitchen, laundry, and breakfast room.
Living, dining, sitting areas.
Bedrooms, baths, utilities.
Garage and storage.

By simple rearrangement of these four units, the house can be made to fit almost any lot, wide or narrow, and oriented properly for any frontage. In this design the units were arranged to obtain the most efficient solar house. It was sketched out from east to west on a wide lot which afforded every solar advantage and privacy for the rear outdoor-living arrangement. In Utah we have four months of outdoor-living weather and eight months of variables and extremes.

All the bedrooms and living areas are on the south. To control the Utah sun to the best possible advantage, the roof is extended over the large glass areas on the south to protect them totally against the solar rays from the last week in April through the second week of August.

A screened terrace off the living room provides a place for the four months of outdoor living. A glass screen or a planting screen or both will be necessary in this area if the terrace is to be used after sundown, because of the strong, cool drafts from the canyons, which in most habitable sections make it uncomfortable to sit outside.

The living, dining, and sitting areas are arranged to enable father and mother and two children to live apart and yet together. The sitting area, with fireplace, is removed from circulation ways and apart from the children's living-play area. For entertaining small groups, the sitting area would be the natural one to use. For large parties the entire living area would be occupied. In a home of this limited size, separation of the sitting area from the rest of the living area saves one generation from being driven out of the house or to bedroom or kitchen while the other entertains.

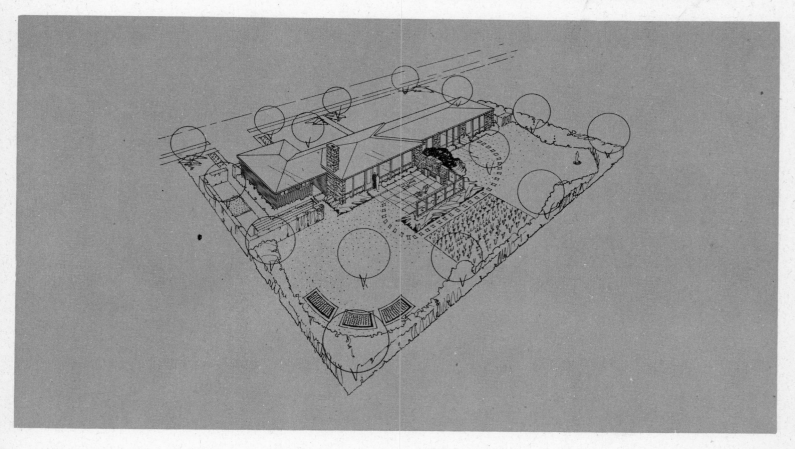

NEVADA

LAURENCE A. GULLING
Architect

NEVADANS love the sun and they love a restful retreat, which too few American homes offer today. The design of this house has two principal objectives: first, to give the solitude-loving Nevadan a maximum of privacy within his own home, and second, to enable him to make the most of the sunshine that bathes this state 79 per cent of the daylight hours.

Most major rooms in the house may be approached from at least two directions. Completely private, and a desirable adjunct to the living room, is the study off the garage hall. Provided with bath facilities, it may readily be used as a guest room.

The arrangement of the dinette is designed to add length to the living room, which in addition to its large sun windows has a clerestory for additional light. This light is reflected from an inclined wall sloping from approximately eight feet up the fireplace wall.

The living-room ceiling has exposed beams on four-foot centers along the underside of the roof, and free *or* exposed beams from beneath the clerestory windows to the inclined-wall intersection.

The brick fireplace, with exposed mirrored breast above the mantel, has a fuel closet to the right and an additional closet, a foot deep, on the opposite side. The hearth is of harmonizing terra cotta. The chimney contains flues for both hot water and the heating system. Screened transoms over each window provide ventilation.

The dinette and kitchen have been placed to receive the morning sun; a house should enable its occupants to start the day off in the most cheerful circumstances possible. The kitchen porch is designed for summertime outside dining.

For kitchen convenience counter space in the form of a "U" has been provided around the double-compartment sink. Additional counter space, with cabinets above, is located at the end of the range and next to the refrigerator.

This house has simple lines, roof with wide exposure, white shingled walls.

The lot is to be graded to produce the effect of lowness for the house.

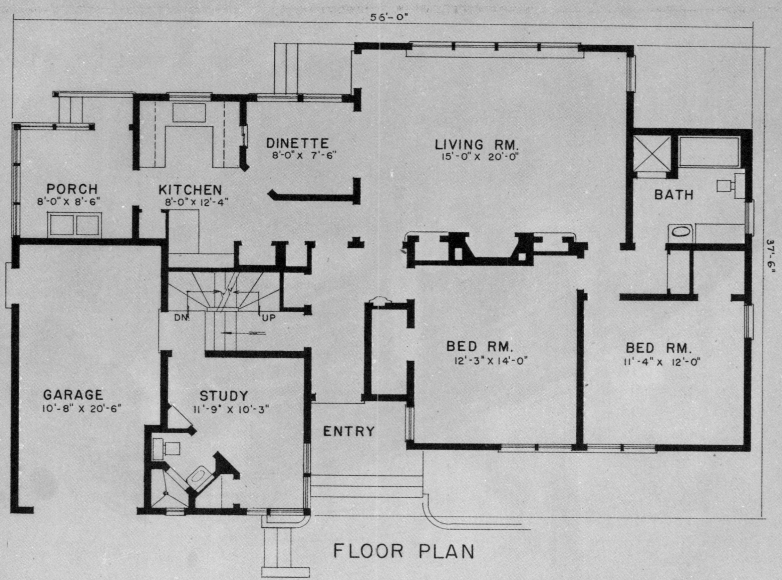

56'-0"

37'-6"

DINETTE
8'-0" x 7'-6"

LIVING RM.
15'-0" x 20'-0"

PORCH
8'-0" x 8'-6"

KITCHEN
8'-0" x 12'-4"

BATH

DN   UP

GARAGE
10'-8" x 20'-6"

STUDY
11'-9" x 10'-3"

BED RM.
12'-3" x 14'-0"

BED RM.
11'-4" x 12'-0"

ENTRY

FLOOR PLAN

117

60.2'

24' × 21'

DR

LR

K

1

2

3

6

U

4

5

7 ®

BR

BR

MBR

B

F

9

32.2'

S Y

16.8'

CP

25.8'

22.2'

1. RANGE
2. REFRIGERATOR
3. DINETTE
4. HOME FREEZER
5. WASHING
6. IRONER
7. BROOMS
8. LINEN
9. COOLER

ARIZONA

RICHARD A. MORSE
Architect

WHATEVER YOU DO for Arizona, always bear this in mind —Arizona is a state of contrasts. Snow blankets its mile-high peaks while cactus blooms in its valleys. Its pine-clad north is cool. Its southern region is a desert. Its roads are traveled by millionaires or by weathered Indian wagons. Its communities range from Indian pueblos to plush resorts as modern as the twenty-first century. Its people are cowhands, miners, ranchers, industrialists, engineers, businessmen, or tourists who stayed on. Their only similarity is in their warmhearted hospitality and their pride of state. Sunlight is dominant,

intensifying the natural colors of the winter landscape or neutralizing them in the incandescence of summer.

In general, rainfall in Arizona is light, humidity is low, the air is clear and dry, the temperature varies from scorching days to cool evenings. Two weather factors largely govern the approach to this solar house—a five-and-a-half-month summer, and a daily temperature range of thirty degrees.

Seasonally, you must heat your house from mid-October to mid-April; the rest of the time you have to exclude heat and direct sunlight. Daily, the temperature is almost constant from 1 P.M. until late afternoon;

the mercury drops rapidly until late at night.

To solve the seasonal problem we devised a simple manual system of roof slides. Around May 1 the slides are extended to exclude direct sunlight; in mid-October they are retracted to readmit the sun.

In consideration of the daily extremes, a controlled eastern exposure was favored, as well as the more standard southern exposure. It also called for elimination of west sunlight at will. This is accomplished by a lowered screen on the east side of the dining bay and by solid masonry at the west wall, pierced for ventilation only by a window with removable outside louvers.

Thirty-five per cent of the solar glass area is designed to open. Although artificial cooling is a daily necessity in the summer, requiring that the house be largely closed during the daytime, the cool of evening allows the opening of glass areas to permit the lower temperature of the night hours to take over. It also is desirable to open the house on the warm days between October and May.

For the Arizona house we favor walls of kiln-baked adobe brick because it is abundant locally and combines insulating qualities with attractive scale and texture. We specify local floor brick in the main living areas and linoleum-covered concrete in the utility sections, for reasons of insulation and resilience.

Exposure of the fireplace to the dining [...] as the living room gives [...]

Flower beds are pla[...] windows not only for d[...] glare. A wind wall on the [...] tion and as a sun trap for w[...] pool and wall fountain ou[...] effect of coolness during h[...]

WASHINGTON

PAUL THIRY
Architect

THE PRINCIPLE, followed here, of a trilevel house with entrance hall giving direct access to all rooms, yields a structure which is compact, easy to maintain, covers a minimum of land area, yet provides sufficient room for the normal functioning of a family of four.

One of the chief considerations influencing the

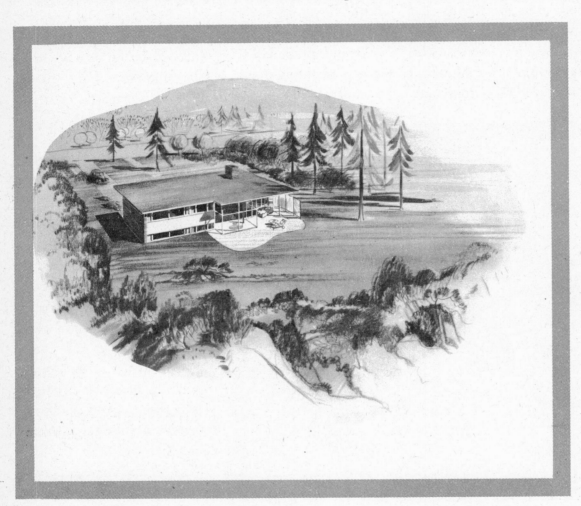

overall design is the extreme variation of climate between the eastern and western parts of the state of Washington. Where one is cold and clear in the winter and the wind is prevalently north, the other is gray and overcast with the prevailing wind southeast to southwest. By like token the one is hot in summer and the other reasonably cool.

Three sides of this structure are practically blanked for privacy and as protection against the weather. The glass areas are principally to the south. The basement, including garage, is abundantly lighted and is as airy [as a]ny room in the house.

[For] simplicity, a flat insulated roof, with single [dra]ining in one direction, is used.

In general, the approach to construction is straightforward. Materials and finishes require a minimum of maintenance.

The living room is reasonably large, has a high ceiling, opens onto the garden and terrace, and has all the characteristics and formality found in a larger house.

In most homes the kitchen is the living center, and as such should be cheerful and comfortable. In this house it is designed as more than a kitchen. It is a place to relax in comfort while meals are on the stove or other work is going forward. There is a fireplace for barbecue or for just plain enjoyment. A door opens to the terrace for dining out. Dinners may be served in the kitchen, or a table may be set in the corner of the living room.

The master bedroom is adjacent to the living room, with which it shares a common sliding wall. At this higher level parents have a retreat from children and yet may supervise their activities unobstrusively. The bedroom thus takes on an air of spaciousness unusual to an otherwise small room.

Bedrooms for children are divided by a folding partition, allowing increased space during the day for play, study, and airing.

The bathroom is divided to provide maximum use, each fixture being in its own cubicle. The utility room provides space for laundry, sewing, and other work, with a closet across the hall for the storage of trunks and hand luggage.

The garage, incorporated into the house, is big enough for two cars, has ample light and generous workbench space, is heated, and has direct access to the entrance hall.

bath

up

dn

kitchen

8'-6" x 16'-0   8'-0" x 16'-0   10'-0" x 16'-0"   16'-0" x 20'-0"

28'-6"

child   child   master

dining

living

FLOOR PLAN

60'-0"

terrace

ENTRANCE ELEVATION, HOUSE FOR LIBBEY OWENS FORD
PIETRO BELLUSCHI, ARCHITECT JUNE 1946

OREGON

PIETRO BELLUSCHI
Architect

OREGON is blessed with magnificent vistas—snow peaks, hills, evergreens, river waterfalls—the things that gladden a man's heart, that he is eager to have as surroundings for his home. With such gifts free for the asking, the designer of a house in Oregon strives mightily to find a way to make their beauty an intimate part of the household's daily experience. The use of large glass areas is the answer to the riddle.

With this foremost in mind, three other considerations appeared to us as basic. First, there must be a generous amount of space devoted to preparation of food and to general utilities. Next, all the mechanical equipment should be concentrated for the sake of economy. Third, the average family, especially where there are children, moves about a house so much that provision must be made to keep the living portion from becoming a passageway for the working and operating portion.

Thus, in this house, the garage is located to give immediate access to the kitchen—an important consideration for the shopping housewife. For this reason a large storage space is provided in the garage itself.

The two bedrooms are placed north, since they are

lived in but little during the day; in addition, many persons want a soft light in their sleeping quarters. During the day the housewife uses the kitchen and utility rooms more than any other part of the house, and they should be sunny and cheerful.

A covered porch outside the utility room is ideally suited for hanging wash and for storage of miscellaneous garden equipment.

A concrete fireplace with fire-brick backing and hearth is provided. High monitor windows give good summer ventilation as well as corridor lighting.

The interior finish is a combination of soft wood, left natural, and plaster which in some places is painted in brilliant colors for interesting accentuation of space. As much furniture as possible should be built in, for conservation of space, utility, and appropriateness.

The principal effect of the interior should be achieved through use of patterns naturally arising from the structure, but handled with restraint for conviction. The exterior materials should be those most readily provided by the locality. This architect's personal preference is for spruce with the rough side out, and Cabot's stain.

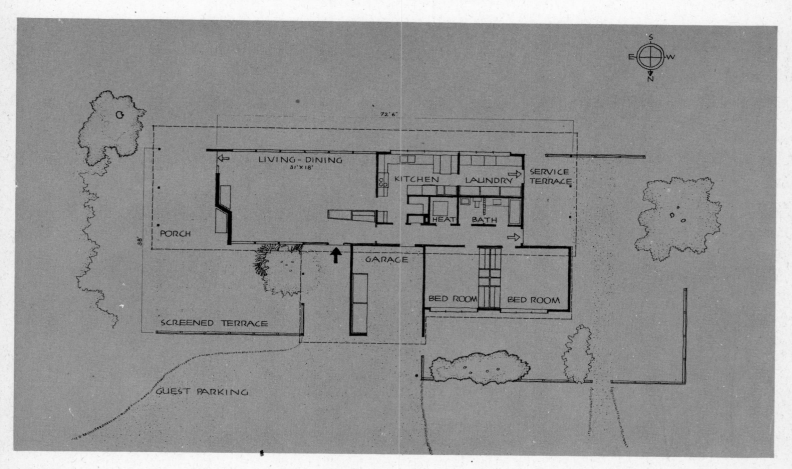

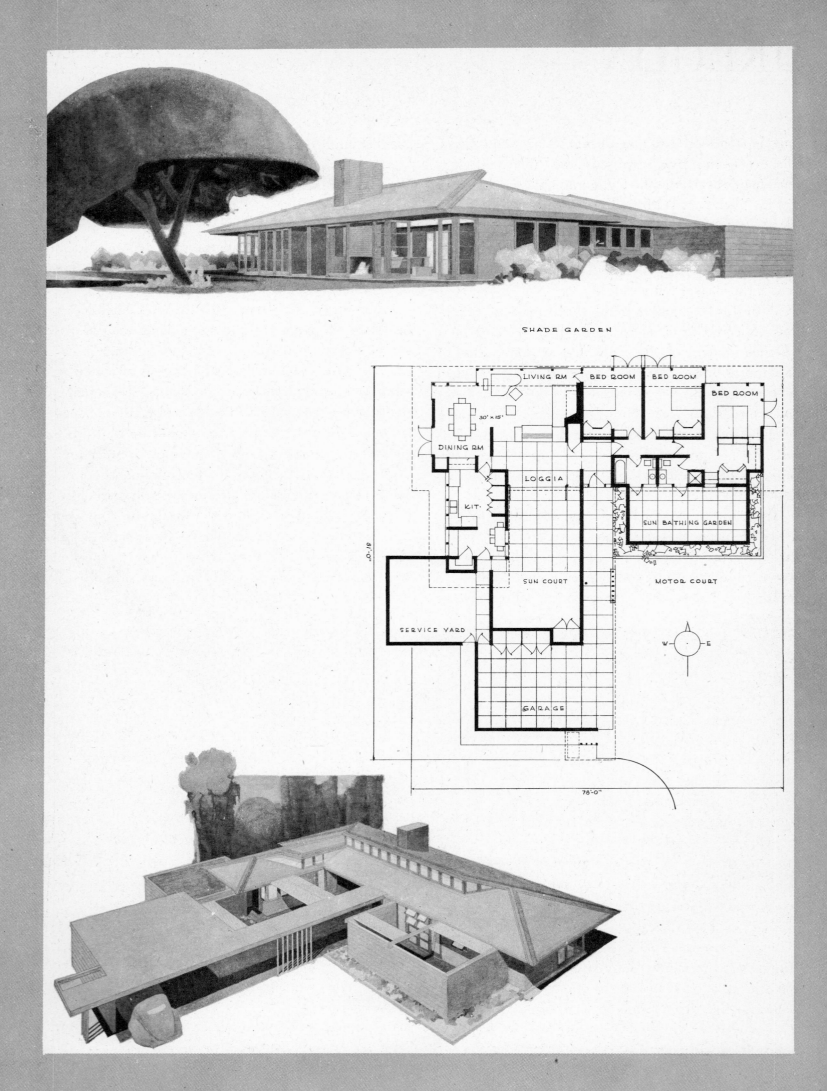

SHADE GARDEN

LIVING RM

BED ROOM

BED ROOM

BED ROOM

DINING RM

30'×15'

LOGGIA

KIT.

SUN BATHING GARDEN

SUN COURT

MOTOR COURT

SERVICE YARD

W E

GARAGE

81'-0"

78'-0"

CALIFORNIA

HARWELL HAMILTON HARRIS
Architect

THANKS to glass, light, like space, has become a flexible element of design. As a consequence we have not only "brought the outside in" and raised the level of illumination, but we have also changed the visual shape of the interior and its atmospheric character.

Perhaps this is easier to do in California than in colder climates. Here there is no need to keep glass out of the north wall and so conserve the heat. If the designer wishes he may make the whole north wall of glass and bring sunlight in through the roof. That is what he has done in this solar house for California. Direct sunlight reaches each room in the house through a continuous band of windows in the roof on the south and east sides.

What does this mean in terms of designing with light?

First of all, the view is on the shady side of the house. The sun is behind you. The sun falls on the back of your neck instead of in your eyes.

Next, illumination is improved. Light from the roof windows spreads evenly over the entire interior, illuminating the tops of objects as well as their sides. The low windows are no longer the only source of illumination; they now are largely view windows.

Third, the shape of the interior is changed. Light entering through the roof has given height—an extension upward—to the interior. In contrast is the effect of the view windows, giving it breadth and extension outward. Placed as they are on opposite sides of the room, these two types of openings create for the beholder a satisfaction that neither alone can provide.

The last effect is an atmospheric one. With the introduction of light from overhead and on at least two sides, there is a loss of solidity. Effects of weight give way to lightness and airiness. A direct ray of sunlight entering through the roof is no longer a knife cutting the darkness and blinding the dweller. In an atmosphere bathed in light it is a golden thread adding sparkle to the pattern. The consideration of such effects is the primary concern of the designer of the solar house. They are principal reasons why a solar house differs from other houses in looks and feel.

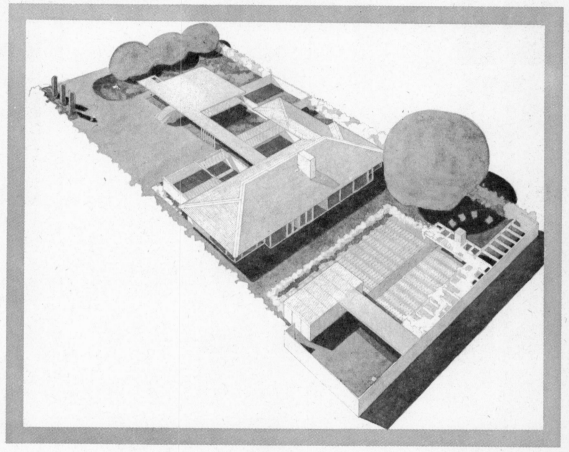

Outside the house, the design calls for shady terraces, warm sun terraces, and private gardens for bathing. On the south side of the loggia is a walled-in sun court. Protected from the breeze, it can be used on sunny days in the very coldest weather. Horizontal panels, resembling sections of a lath house roof, slide the full length of the co   en an overhead track. They may be used to shade t shade the garden cour

The three sections a large patch of shade vide smaller patches. court, they form the toward the loggia.

Another garden i reached directly from

ARCHITECTS

ARMSTRONG, Harris
3 Sappington Spur,
Kirkwood, Mo.

BECHTEL, Harold E.
55½ Broadway,
Fargo, N. D.

BELLUSCHI, Pietro
2040 S. W. Jefferson
Street,
Portland, Ore.

BRIGHAM, Norman R.
Keeline Building,
Omaha, Neb.

BURKS, H. Ray
Burks and Anderson,
502 Wallace Building,
Little Rock, Ark.

CERNY, Robert G.
Long & Thorshov, Inc.,
1200 Second Avenue,
South
Minneapolis, Minn.

CUSHING, Ralph H.
Cushing & Terrell,
Box 1372,
Billings, Mont.
Associate:
Everett O. Terrell

DOW, Alden B.
Alden B. Dow, Inc.,
315 Post Street,
Midland, Mich.

EMERY, Amos B.
715 Locust Street,
Des Moines, Iowa

FORD, O'Neil
Ford, Swank & Rogers,
Route 7, Willow Way,
San Antonio, Tex.
Associates:
Gerald R. Rogers,
San Antonio;
A. B. Swank,
Dallas, Tex.

FORDYCE, Allmon
Glen Gardner, N. J.

FREEMAN, Ruth
Reynolds
Freeman, French &
Freeman,
138 Church Street,
Burlington, Vt.
Associates:
William W. Freeman,
John C. French, Jr.

GULLING, Laurence A.
Gulling & Means,
217 Clay Peters
Building,
Reno, Nev.

GUNTHER, John
Peterborough, N. H.,
Deceased (See
Philip Rogers)

HARKNESS, Albert
1428 Industrial Trust
Building,
Providence, R. I.

HARMON, G. Thomas,
III
236 South Harden
Street,
Moultrieville, S. C.

HARRIS, Harwell H.
2311 Fellowship
Parkway,
Los Angeles, Cal.

HAYS, J. Byers
Conrad, Hays, Simpson
& Ruth,
1110 Hanna Building,
Cleveland, Ohio
Associates:
Edward G. Conrad,
Russell Simpson,
Paul C. Ruth

HIGGINS, Ambrose S.
Bar Harbor, Me.

HOMSEY, Victorine and
Samuel
917 Gilpin Avenue,
Wilmington, Del.

HOYT, Burnham
400 Colorado National
Bank Building,
Denver, Colo.

JAMISON, T. Worth, Jr.
Jamison & Marcks,
8 East Mulberry Street,
Baltimore, Md.
Associate:
E. Russell Marcks

KAESER, William V.
2306 University
Avenue,
Madison, Wis.

KAMPHOEFNER,
Henry L.
School of Architecture,
University of
Oklahoma,
Norman, Okla.

KASTNER, Alfred
1528 Connecticut
Avenue, N. W.,
Washington, D. C.

KECK, George Fred
612 N. Michigan
Avenue,
Chicago, Ill.

KOCH, Richard
907 Queen & Crescent
Building,
New Orleans, La.
Associate:
Samuel Wilson, Jr.

KOCHER, A. Lawrence
Coke-Garrett House,
Williamsburg, Va.
Associates:
Louis W. Ballou,
Charles C Justice

MALVANEY, Edgar L.
Millsaps Building,
Jackson, Miss.

MARTENS, Walter F.
Martens & Son,
301 United Carbon
Building,
Charleston, W. Va.
Associate:
Robert E. Martens

MEEM, John Gaw
P. O. Box 628,
Santa Fe, N. M.

MORSE, Richard A.
Morse and Peters,
3227 North First
Avenue,
Tucson, Ariz.
Associate:
William Y. Peters

OBERWARTH, C. Julian
301 Second Street,
Frankfort, Ky.
Associates:
William C. Livingston,
Jr., J. Leland Brewster

ORR, Douglas
96 Grove Street,
New Haven, Conn.

PARRISH, Lowell E.
423 Beneficial Life
Building,
Salt Lake City, Utah

PEARSON, Clyde C.
Clyde C. Pearson and
Farrow L. Tittle,
412 First National Bank
Building,
Montgomery, Ala.
Associate:
Farrow L. Tittle

PORTER, Frederic H.
2118 Central Avenue,
Cheyenne, Wyo.
Associate:
R. Walter Bradley

PRICHARD, Theodore
Jan
Box 211,
University Post Office,
Moscow, Idaho

ROGERS, Phillip
Hardwick, Worcester
County, Mass.
(For John Gunther,
Peterborough, N. H.,
Deceased)

SPITZNAGEL, Harold
National Bank of
South Dakota
Building,
Sioux Falls, S. D.
Associate:
John A. Schoening

STUBBINS, Hugh, Jr.
1430 Massachusetts
Avenue,
Cambridge, Mass.

ROWLAND, John J.
330 North Queen
Street,
Kinston, N. C.

STEVENS, Preston S.
Stevens & Wilkinson, Inc.,
157 Luckie St., N.W.,
Atlanta, Ga.

THIRY, Paul
1331 Third Avenue
Building,
Seattle, Wash.

SMITH, J. Frazer
J. Frazer Smith, Inc.,
Suite 404,
Goodwyn Institute,
Memphis, Tenn.

STONE, Edward D.
Edward D. Stone
Associates,
50 E. 64th Street,
New York, N. Y.
Associates:
Stanley C. Reece,
Alexander Knowlton,
J. Graham Stewart,
Karl J. Holzinger, Jr.

WEED, Robert Law
The Office of
Robert Law Weed,
1527 duPont Building,
Miami, Fla.
Associates:
Frank H. Shuflin,
T. Trip Russell,
Frank E. Watson

SCHMIDT, Lorentz
Lorentz Schmidt,
McVay & Peddie,
1832 East Second
Street,
Wichita, Kan.
Associates:
Wayne M. McVay,
Thomas H. Peddie

STONOROV, Oscar G.,
and KAHN, Louis I.
Associated Architects,
Bulletin Building,
Philadelphia, Pa.

WRIGHT, John Lloyd
Beach Club
Apartments,
La Jolla, Calif.
(Formerly residing at
Long Beach, Michigan
City, Ind.)